Southwestern Flying Adventures

James S. Kohn, M.D.

PETER E. RANDALL PUBLISHER
Portsmouth, New Hampshire
2003

Library of Congress Control Number: 2003091251
ISBN: 1-931807-14-0

Design and maps: Grace Peirce

Peter E. Randall Publisher
Box 4726
Portsmouth, NH 03802
www.perpublisher.com

Distributed by University Press of New England
Hanover and London

To those who made this book possible,
most notably my trusting passengers;
my patient transcriptionist, Michelle,
and my lovely little wife, Gwen.

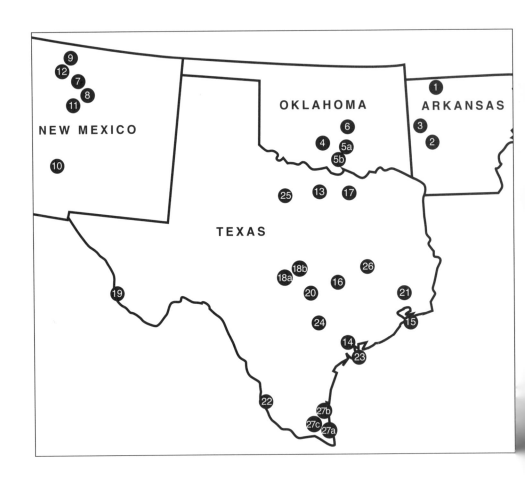

Contents

Introduction

I am neither a native of the Southwest nor an expert on the region, but I have a true love for both aviation and exploring. If you share these passions, you will find this guide useful and fun. It will help you plan your adventures, leaving less to chance and disappointment, and affording you more time and energy to see and do great things at your destination. Let's face it, as general aviation pilots, we all love to be in command, but part of the responsibility as commander of an expedition is to be social director! As a rule, we love to fly, even with no destination in mind, but companionship is essential and making a great day out of a great flight is an art.

This guide will help you make the most out of your travels. It is a compilation of my own experiences, days and weekends spent over the last several years. In some cases I have chosen a particular destination because it offers a unique activity or sight to see. It is a guide for the young at heart and the adventurous, for those who may want to stray a bit from the beaten path. The goal is to sustain the least amount of inconvenience in doing this, and to learn from mistakes that I have made!

For this reason, the flights are cross-referenced by attraction and by location. If you wake up early on Sunday morning with a desire to go horseback riding, proceed to the attractions appendix. If you need to get out of the Texas summer heat for an upcoming weekend, then plan a couple of days at altitude in New Mexico. This guide should serve as a springboard to facilitate and encourage new adventures that are your own. Use it for ideas and as a starting point, as well as for the specific tips and references. I've included a few maps for some of the more remote airports where you may not encounter anyone on the ground (i.e., no FBO). These maps are not drawn to scale.

I have tried to make the information in this guide as accurate as possible, but mistakes are inevitable. I apologize in advance for any of these inaccuracies, especially if they adversely affect your trip. If you e-mail or write me of any corrections or suggestions, you are sure to get a response, and a thank-you at the very least! I have come to recognize that being a pilot is virtually an automatic induction into a fraternal organization that involves help in need, respect, and camaraderie. I love meeting those who share this attitude and have learned from the advice and experiences of others. This is one of the main reasons I have written this guide. Best wishes on your flying adventures.

jameskohn@worldnet.att.net

Glen and Evelyn beside their Maule. See page 3 for a closer look.

Planning Your Adventure: Transportation Once You Get There

One of the major challenges in venturing out and about small airports is a lack of ground transportation once you have landed. I have had to be a bit daring in the several years since I started venturing from remote airfields. For example, accepting rides from strangers might raise the eyebrows of many concerning safety and just plain old good judgment. But taxi service can be unpredictable and unreliable, as can rental or loaner car service. I would like to share a couple of experiences to illustrate the point.

There was a loaner car at the airport in Las Vegas, New Mexico (see page 33) in which the front-end alignment was so bad that the vibration was unbearable above a speed of 30 miles per hour. Unfortunately, one Sunday I found myself driving this vehicle several miles away from our point of interest, the Gallinas Canyon trailhead, when I realized the mechanical limitations of our free ride and that the last 4 or 5 miles was a steep mountain road with hairpin turns! "Not too smart, doc," was all I could say to myself. To make matters worse, the brakes on this 1970s Oldsmobile were marginally functional. We crept along at about 10 miles per hour and finally made it to the trailhead deep in the woods. A jump start was necessary for our return trip just as dusk was approaching. Luckily, the only other vehicle in the parking lot had cables.

The moral of the story is that loaner cars at small airports should be carefully scrutinized for anything more than a 2-mile round-trip. Never look a gift horse in the mouth, but asking for dental records is not a bad idea!

My second vignette involves the use of bicycles on an August afternoon in southern Oklahoma. I love bicycling and I own three foldable cycles, two with 16-inch wheels and one a full-size mountain bike. I can fit the two small Dahon "folders" in the baggage compartment, leaving the four seats of my Mooney for passengers. Alternatively, I can remove the rear seat backs (or fold them forward) to accommodate two standard-size mountain bikes or two road bikes. These have to be loaded through the passenger door (not the rear baggage compartment door), and the wheels (both front and rear) must be removed. Even an extra-large frame will fit. The two frames go in first and the four wheels follow. Ground cloths are a good idea to prevent grease on the leather and upholstery.

Two Dahon folders (background left) and the Diblasi motorized scooter (foreground).

In this sad tale, I miscalculated the distance to a refreshment stop in 108-degree heat and 90 percent humidity. I might add that my guest was not as enthusiastic as I was about cycling and had a particular distaste for hilly terrain. Being a Texan, I think she probably did not like Oklahoma either—perhaps one of those football rivalry things. After the first few miles I was feeling that her glare was more oppressive than the afternoon sun. It took forever to reach our destination, which was supposedly just up the road a way.

The moral of this story is twofold: Try to gather as much information from the locals about the area surrounding the airport and never underestimate or exceed the thermostat of a Texas woman!

For the less energetic, there are some really great motorized vehicles on the market. They aren't cheap, but then nothing is that's made to complement vehicles of luxury like yachts and aircraft. The willingness to assemble and disassemble these modes of transportation, the available space and weight limitations, and your budget and sense of adventure are the main factors to consider. Some examples are listed below, including illustrations of custom-rigged aircraft.

Custom-rigged aircraft.

I met Glen and Evelyn on Sunday afternoon at Possum Kingdom airport in Texas. They were unloading a Honda 70 cc scooter from their Maule aircraft using an ingeniously designed ramp. The motorized bike fit perfectly into a space behind the two front seats without the need for any disassembly or modification. They rolled it to the ground in seconds and sped off into the countryside (see photo). Another option for motorized transportation is the DiBlasi folding scooter. This product has the advantage of relatively low weight (64 pounds) with a remarkable small profile in the folded state. Folding is quick and easy and no disassembly is necessary. It is rated to carry 320 pounds, but should be considered a one-person mode of transportation due to the size of the seat. Check the Web site at www.Diblasi.com for specifications, prices, and other information.

ARKANSAS

The runway surface and parking area at Gaston's Airfield.

Gaston's, Arkansas
(Lakeview, AK 3MO)

Location: Northern Arkansas, amid the Ozark Mountains

Airfield: Gaston's Airfield is a 3,200-foot turf strip, privately owned but open to the public for general aviation use. The soft field sits next to Gaston's Resort, a premier trout-fishing institution that has been featured in AOPA and other flying magazines.

For a grass strip, this field is extremely well-kept up, but the following precautions should be taken. First, understand that the landing surface is in a valley surrounded by some nonthreatening peaks. This has benefits, but it imposes difficulties as well. One benefit to being in a valley is significant shelter from prevailing winds and wind shear. The difficulties arise from ground fog, the need for a relatively steep approach (a high angle of attack), and in this case, the rising terrain just beyond the end of runway 06. For this reason, most pilots land in the direction of runway 24 and take off in the direction of runway 06 unless strong headwinds prevail.

One more idiosyncrasy about this field is worthy of note. On runway 24 there is a slight rise just after touchdown which will probably cause you to become airborne shortly after landing. If you anticipate this, it may alleviate some of your anxiety and also provide you with the opportunity to make two good landings!

As mentioned, the field is well maintained and there is very little debris that could take you by surprise. By calling Gaston's Resort, however, someone will be happy to provide you with specific information, such as who has recently landed and how much rain the field has absorbed over the past day or so.

This is an excellent place to practice soft-field takeoffs and landings as well. The field gets quite a bit of use on Saturday and Sunday mornings, however, as many folks will come for a short trip, brunch, or lunch. White wooden markers outline the width of the field and mark its length. These would do considerable damage to any landing aircraft, so please be careful and don't aim for them. Ground services at the strip are provided by the resort staff. They are eager to help and have many vehicles to help you tote luggage or passengers who may require extra assistance. My experience at Gaston's is noteworthy for unprecedented hospitality and accommodations.

My first mate and crew! Trout fishing along the White River at Gaston's resort.

Attractions:

Fishing, hiking, boating

Description: Gaston's Resort in northern Arkansas is a must for any general aviation pilot who loves fishing and the outdoors, or who has always wanted to visit the White River or the Ozarks. The experience offers the opportunity to practice safe landings and build confidence in soft-field operations.

The resort itself is neither pretentious nor contrived. It offers down-home cooking in rustic elegance and an easygoing atmosphere. A trip to Gaston's Airfield is really a trip to the restaurant and/or the White River for fishing, hiking, and just relaxing. The accommodations range from single, hotel-like rooms to cabins that can house a large family. Most of these have their own fireplaces, and all look out onto the White River. Trout fishing by riverboat is by far the most popular activity at Gaston's, but other activities are available. There is a 2-mile nature trail as well as a tennis court and swimming pool right at the grounds. As

The White River at Gaston's resort, dusk.

expected, the busiest time here is fall, during the change of seasons when the soft shades of red, brown, and yellow surround you for a few weeks. At other times of the year you will be guaranteed seclusion, privacy, and less river traffic.

The restaurant at Gaston's is outstanding, and will satisfy the discriminating palate as well as those who prefer down-home cooking. The wine selection is extensive and the surroundings are casual. You'll enjoy your meal while sitting in the main dining room, which overlooks the White River some 50 feet below. The decor is quite interesting and eye-catching. Antique bicycles and boating equipment including weathered outboard motors are suspended from the ceiling and walls. Gaston's Restaurant offers breakfast, lunch, and dinner daily, and features a spectacular brunch on weekends. Take advantage of this brunch—it costs only $12.95 and guarantees you won't eat for a week afterward!

The town of Bull Shoals is a small lakeside community, just a couple of miles from the resort. There is a restaurant here that is quite good, but the main reason for venturing into town is to pick up groceries or other supplies. Gaston's Resort has a small shop for basic supplies and sundries, but no provisions for making a large meal for your family or friends. Many folks take advantage of the fact that most cabins are equipped with a full kitchen as well as a barbecue outside. Included in the price of your accommodations is the use of a boat from the riverside marina. The long, narrow fishing boats are quite comfortable and geared to this stretch of the White River. They draw very little water and hold three people safely. Although your room comes with a boat, motor rentals are approximately $50 a day. Fishing rod, tackle, and guide rentals are also available. The river is famous for trout and serves as a gathering for anglers of all abilities. On any given spring or summer day you will find expert fly fishermen sharing the waters with those using simple gear and live bait. It all seems to work out nicely as there is plenty of river to share and explore.

When You Go:

Spend a little time familiarizing yourself with the approach to runway 24 and the surrounding area by looking over your VFR chart, and call ahead to research the field conditions. Alternatively, you can land at either of two lengthy, paved municipal airports if you prefer to avoid soft-field conditions. The closer is Marion County Regional (FLP) and the other is Baxter County. Both are easily approached and offer runways in excess of 4,000 feet. Gaston's Resort staff will pick you up at either upon request.

Take some friends to Gaston's for a weekend of fishing and fun. Bring a cooler of your favorite snacks and take advantage of the wonderful picnic facilities as well as the fully equipped cabins. Arrange an outing or a caravan of your aviation buddies. Plan on at least brunch at their riverside restaurant Saturday or Sunday morning.

Contacts:

Gaston's Resort	(870) 431-5202
Marion County Regional Airport	(870) 453-2241
Baxter County Airport	(870) 481-5966
Flippen Airport	(870) 453-2241

Hot Springs, Arkansas (HOT)

Location: South-central Arkansas, within the Ouachita National Forest

Airfield: Hot Springs Memorial Field is an ideal destination for the general aviation pilot. This airport is uncontrolled, yet a significant amount of commercial and commuter activity takes place here. Recent renovations of the main runway, as well as a new terminal building, have given the field a facelift. The larger of two runways is 6,600 feet, and the approach is unobstructed at either end. There are a few hills to the north, but there is nothing in the way of major obstacles or hazards. The field is quite close to major areas of recreation and the town is just a few miles away.

Ground transportation from Hot Springs Memorial Field is relatively easy. A loaner car is available, but heavily used on a first-come, first-served basis. There are taxi services, too, and a Hertz Rental Agency is based at the main terminal building. Hertz is open seven days a week. In addition, several of the hotels and bed-and-breakfasts will arrange to pick you up at the airport.

The approach to Hot Springs, Arkansas. Left base to final, runway 5.

Newly surfaced Hot Springs memorial Airport.

Attractions:
Historical points of interest (the springs), Lake Ouachita, Lake Hamilton (houseboats), hiking in the Ouachita National Forest, horseback riding

Description: Hot Springs is a great weekend getaway. The city is small and quiet enough to have maintained its charm and relaxed ambience, yet convenient in terms of amenities and accessibility. Tourist attractions focus on the natural resources of the area's lakes and beautiful forests, as well as the hot springs and bathing houses developed in the early twentieth century. These facilities are still in use today, but perhaps have become overshadowed by the fact that this small metropolis is the hometown of former president Bill Clinton. Nearly all of the shops and restaurants have signed photographs of President Clinton and the first lady: The people are quite proud of their hometown boy.

Central Avenue in downtown Hot Springs is the center of tourism. The visitors center here is quite helpful and provides an unbiased directory to restaurants, activities, and accommodations. At one end of this thoroughfare is the Arlington Resort and Spa. This grand hotel is clearly the most well known in town. President Clinton is said to have stayed here on more than one occasion, and the structure itself is monumental. On Saturday nights, there is dancing, and the pool and spa are famous. A visit to the lobby for drinks or hors d'oeuvres is well worth it even if you are not staying here. Many other choices for accommodations are more serene and picturesque, including lakeside establishments. Prices vary, but are generally reasonable.

If you'd like to try houseboat accommodations, this is a great opportunity. Lake Ouachita is ideally set up for this activity. The waters are glassy and calm, with few hazards. A 2- to 3-day voyage about this 50-mile lake will prove to be a memorable experience. If you are not the boating type but still would like to enjoy the beautiful shores of Lake Ouachita, other options are listed below. Hiking, horseback riding, or other land-based activities are widely advertised and easy to arrange from one of the many resorts that surround Lake Ouachita and Lake Hamilton. All of these are accessible by car and within a 45-minute drive.

When You Go:

Choose a weekend in the early fall to visit Hot Springs, and invite two to four of your closest friends to share a houseboat with you. Prearrange this adventure with the Brady Mountain Resort just a 15-minute drive from the airport. Plan for a few days of lakeside activity—and bring your video camera.

Alternatively, fly to Hot Springs for an overnight. Stay in the Arlington Hotel and eat brunch at Sinks. Sinks is an eclectic restaurant located on the top floor of a small shopping plaza in the heart of town. It has wonderful pancakes and monster salads. Take a stroll past the bathhouses and even go into one to enjoy some of the medicinal qualities of this local pastime. If you stay at the Arlington, this establishment has its own hot spring just adjacent to the pool.

Make sure you stop by the visitors center to ensure that you have not missed a particular interest of your own.

Contacts:

Hot Springs Memorial Airport	(501) 321-6750
Hertz Rental Car	(501) 623-7591
Arlington Resort Hotel and Spa	(800) 643-1502;
	(501) 623-7771
www.arlingtonhotel.com	
Brady Mountain Houseboat Rental	(501) 760-2659
Brady Mountain Resort	(501) 767-6506
Klein Shore Resort (charming	
lakeside accommodations)	(501) 767-5020

Mena, Arkansas (M39)

Location: In southwest Arkansas, nestled within a ridge of 2,000- to 3,000-foot mountains. The town is just outside of the Ouachita Forest, 50 miles south of Fort Smith.

Airfield: Mena Intermountain Airfield is a surprisingly large, two-runway field that gets remarkably little use. When you approach the field, you will be surprised at how many large jets are on the ground lined up as if this were a major commercial airport. There are several aircraft maintenance companies based here, which accounts for the number of idle jets awaiting service. This is not a busy place, however, and despite its position among the hills and small mountains, it's an easy place to get in and out of for the novice general aviation pilot.

At the general aviation terminal, you will see indications of many pilots who made this spot their first solo destination. This fact attests to the ease and safety of landing here. The intersecting runways are 6,000 and 4,000 feet respectively, 100 feet wide, and well maintained. There is no tower and, in fact, I was unable to raise anyone at the FBO on the radio for advisories on approach. Although the typical services are available for an uncontrolled airport (fuel, phone, and restroom), this place is quiet with a capital Q!

Rental cars can be arranged weekdays by the local Ford dealership, Mena Ford. This service is reliable and the rates are quite reasonable. Service is available on weekends, if arrangements are made ahead.

Attractions:

Horseback riding, hiking, walking, leaf peeping

Description: Mena Intermountain Airfield is the gateway to a relaxing fall weekend in southern Arkansas. These mountains are not the Ozarks, but they are quite lovely and at certain times of the year approach New England in beauty with respect to fall foliage; the colors are softer, but the landscapes are splendid nonetheless. This is a nice place to spend a weekend in October.

The town of Mena is not particularly interesting. There is one restaurant I would recommend for dinner (the Chopping Block), and the hotels are affordable, but certainly not luxurious. The Queen Wilhelmena Lodge is approximately 14 miles from the airport. This establishment sits atop the mountain ridge in a scenic setting. It is an Arkansas State-owned

The airport at Mena, Arkansas—eerily quiet!

resort with a family-style atmosphere. There are some wonderful nature walks here, nothing too strenuous. Not far away you can arrange for horseback riding or swimming at Lake Mena or some of the other popular spots.

When You Go:

Make reservations for the Queen Wilhelmena Lodge well ahead. Choose a weekend in October and prearrange for a rental car. Lodging is your main concern, as fall foliage weekends get filled up months in advance. Have dinner just outside of Mena at the Chopping Block, south of town on Route 71. (The food is better here than at the lodge.) Take your time along the 14-mile drive leading to the lodge from town. Bring your camera to enjoy the best of the region's fall foliage. When you get to the lodge, take a walk on one of the many well-marked trails. Ask the folks at the front desk to provide you with a map. For me, they demonstrated true and tremendous hospitality. Although this place isn't fancy, it's very comfortable.

Contacts:

Mena Intermountain Municipal Airfield (main number and FBO)	(501) 394-4077
Queen Wilhelmena Lodge	(501) 394-2863
Sun Country Inn	(501) 394-7477
Mena Ford (car rental)	(501) 394-2214
Chopping Block Restaurant	(501) 394-6410

OKLAHOMA

The northern shore of Lake Murray has trails for off-road cycling.

Lake Murray State Park, Oklahoma (1F1)

Location: Lake Murray is a resort area 20 miles to the west of Lake Texoma, the largest lake in southern Oklahoma/northern Texas. Lake Murray Airfield is listed as Overbrook in the AFD.

Airfield: The landing strip at Lake Murray is 2,500 feet long by 50 feet wide with a few cracks in it. The best landmarks to identify the field are the golf course just to the south of it and the lakeside resort to the north. The approach is not difficult, but the up-slope of runway 14 is a perceptual aberration that should be anticipated. There are no services at the landing strip per se, but 50 yards away is the golf course pro shop. The folks here are helpful and will provide information about the surrounding area and communication with the Lake Murray State Resort. A shuttle van is usually available for transportation from the airstrip to the resort, half a mile away. Cold drinks, snacks, and rest rooms can also be found at the golf course pro shop.

Chain tie-downs at the airfield will secure your plane, but make no mistake, there is no supervision or airport surveillance here. This is a small, uncontrolled airport with no instrument approach. However, the Ardmore Oklahoma Downtown Municipal Airport is 5 miles down the road to the northwest. Fuel and services (including an FBO) are available here. Transportation options from Ardmore are also limited but instrument approaches are possible and the runway is long, smooth, and well maintained, making it an excellent alternative in marginal weather or when a longer, wider landing surface is necessary.

Attractions:

Golf, water sports at the lake, restaurants, nature walks, mountain biking, horseback riding

Description: Lake Murray State Park and Resort is an area surrounding Lake Murray, and is run and owned by the state of Oklahoma. The resort hotel, which is lakefront, is approximately 1/2 mile from the airstrip. Rooms are available in the main building as well as in lakeside cabins. These are a bit more private and suited to young families.

Each time I visit Lake Murray, I'm struck by the fact that the water differs greatly in color from Lake Texoma, about 20 miles to the east.

Equestrian activities are popular in southern Oklahoma.

The brownish green waters of Texoma are in striking contrast to the blue and more clear waters of Lake Murray. Lake Murray is only a fraction of the size of Texoma, but there is still little traffic on the lake. The sense of serenity and escape can be found here much of the time. A marina adjacent to the hotel has kayaks, paddleboats, and wave runners for rent, and a larger marina, about 1 mile down the road, serves as the center of watercraft activities.

Separate from the resort, there are two restaurants within walking distance of the airfield. One is a down-home luncheon place, Callaway's, that specializes in catfish. This is genuine Oklahoma to its core and perfect for a quick lunch, a 7-minute walk from your tie-down. The Fireside is great for dinner. This restaurant is family-style as well, but with more elegant decor and atmosphere. The Fireside specializes in prime rib but occasionally sells out, especially on a Saturday night. Reservations are not usually necessary, however.

Finally, just adjacent to the entrance to the state park resort (see map) are riding stables. Horse trails wind through the woods and make for an enjoyable 1- to 2-hour family activity. Nature trails and picnic areas surround the resort, perfect for small children or Scouts. Bicycles can be rented at the resort, but beware, they are in various states of disrepair!

The Lake Murray outing is neither an extravagant nor a luxurious experience, but it can be a wonderful getaway that is simply and affordably enjoyable.

A vignette will illustrate the hospitable nature of one local police officer at Lake Murray. On an evening prior to my departure from the active runway, this young man had spotted me and my copilot and signaled us to wait at the tie-down area. It was dusk and the runway lights were barely noticeable when he proceeded to race twice up and down the runway in his patrol car with high beams and searchlight. He chased two deer from the strip and sent them frolicking into a nearby meadow. He then drove off the runway and, with a smile, motioned us to take the active.

When You Go:

Plan a weekend trip and bring your children. Take them on a nature walk through the wooded area adjacent to the lake and bring some fishing poles. In the evening, take a swim at the resort or even rent a boat at the marina to explore some of the coves of this lake.

The golf course adjacent to the airstrip is a good place to learn the game. It is seldom crowded and the greens fees are more than reasonable ($14 on the weekends for eighteen holes). If you ever want to teach someone to play golf, this is an ideal place. Have lunch at Callaway's and dinner at The Fireside. You might even want to practice a few short field landings and takeoffs at this quiet airstrip.

Contacts:

Ardmore Aviation (FBO at	
Ardmore Executive Airport)	(580) 223-8172
Lake Murray Resort	(580) 223-6600
Callaway's Catfish Restaurant	(580) 226-1648
The Fireside Restaurant	(580) 226-4070
Lake Murray Golf Course	(580) 223-6613
The Riding Stables	(580) 223-8172

Lake Texoma State Park, Oklahoma (F31)/Cedar Mills, Oklahoma (3T0)

Location: Lake Texoma State Park Airport is adjacent to the largest lake in Texas, which gets its name from *Tex*as and Oklah*oma*. The airport is technically in Oklahoma, but the state line runs through the mid-portion of the lake.

Airfield: The airport is just southwest of a golf course, making it easier to identify on the approach. This 3,000-foot paved strip is oriented north–south, like many of the other runways in this area, to accommodate the prevailing breeze, most commonly out of the south. Beware of a slight downslope to runway 18. Nonetheless, there are no major obstacles to contend with and the VFR sectional chart, Dallas/Fort Worth, provides some handy landmarks for identification.

There is no fuel at the field and courtesy car availability is unreliable. Your best option for transportation is a prearranged lift from your home-base accommodations. The state resort cabins are within walking distance of the parking area and courtesy vans are available as well. You can call the resort from the courtesy phone at the tie-down area.

A second airfield at Lake Texoma is Cedar Mills (3T0). This soft lakeside field is 10 miles south of Lake Texoma State Park Airstrip and features a 3,000-foot-long by 60-foot-wide turf/grass surface. Field conditions are variable, but an update on specifics can be obtained by calling the resort at which this field is based. Depending on whom you contact at the time, the information can be very helpful. As mentioned, Cedar Mills Field is within walking distance of the resort, and of lakeside dining as well.

Attractions:
Fishing, boating, watersports, hiking, walking, golf

Description: Lake Texoma is a consequence of the Army Corps of Engineers' work in damming up the Red River, a natural dividing line between Texas and Oklahoma. The lake is a popular recreational area for folks who live nearby. It is a fairly shallow lake in most parts with murky and muddy waters. Much of the convoluted shoreline is barren, but a few houses and resorts are scattered along the shores. It rarely

Lake Texoma State park, approach to Runway 36.

becomes crowded due to the sheer length of its projections, which span more than 30 miles in the shape of a U.

If you are a fisherman and are even remotely familiar with this area, you will note the reputation Texoma has for striped bass. This species was transplanted to its landlocked state many years ago, and now has flourished. Fully equipped and guided charters can be easily arranged to enjoy this activity.

Several small towns are scattered along the lake. Kingston is the closest to Lake Texoma Airport, 4 miles to the west, and Gordonville is 3 miles from Cedar Mills. These towns are small, unsophisticated, and typical of rural Oklahoma. There is not much to see here in the way of history or culture; the experience is purely natural/recreational. Lake Texoma Airport abuts an eighteen-hole golf course, an easy day outing, with no need for ground transfer. Cedar Mills is great for an afternoon lunch or brunch fly-in to the Pelican Landing, a lakeside restaurant. The resort is excellent for an overnight getaway as well.

When You Go:

Plan a trip to Texoma for a striper fishing expedition for you and your passengers. The spring and fall are preferable because of the often

Aerial view of the soft field landing surface at Cedar Mills.

stifling heat associated with midsummer in this region. The most convenient accommodations are at the state-owned resort, abutting the airport. Alternatively, you can stay at the Tanglewood, perhaps the nicest resort around. A memorable weekend could also involve renting a houseboat at Willow Springs. The best way to see the lake at your leisure is by renting a motorboat from one of the many marinas that scatter the shoreline. Or, a day trip to the Texoma area might involve lunch and a stroll around Cedar Mills. Remember to inquire about field conditions before you go, preferably from someone who is well informed, at the resort.

Contacts:

Lake Texoma State Park Airport	(405) 375-4886
Cedar Mills Resort (on the field)	(903) 523-4222
Lake Texoma Resort	(580) 564-2311
Tanglewood Resort	(903) 786-2968
Denison Chamber of Commerce	(903) 465-1551
Willow Springs Houseboat Rentals	(580) 924-6240
Striped Bass Fishing Charters	(800) 211-7808

Tishomingo, Oklahoma (0F9)

Location: Southwestern Oklahoma, not far from Lake Texoma

Airfield: Tishomingo Airpark is a quiet, 3,100-foot paved strip surrounded by a nature preserve. There is a large lake just southeast of the strip that serves as a good landmark. The surrounding area is wooded, but there are few hazards here and the visual approach is straightforward. There are no phones and no services at the airport area. Some dilapidated hangars occupy the east side of the runway. These are next to what seems to be the caretaker's trailer.

Attractions:
Nature walks, hunting, biking

Description: I have included Tishomingo in this guide for one specific reason: This airfield is one of the few I came across that features the ability to hunt from your plane without the need for ground

Hangars and parking area at the Tishomingo Airport (construction needed!).

Tishomingo (0F9)

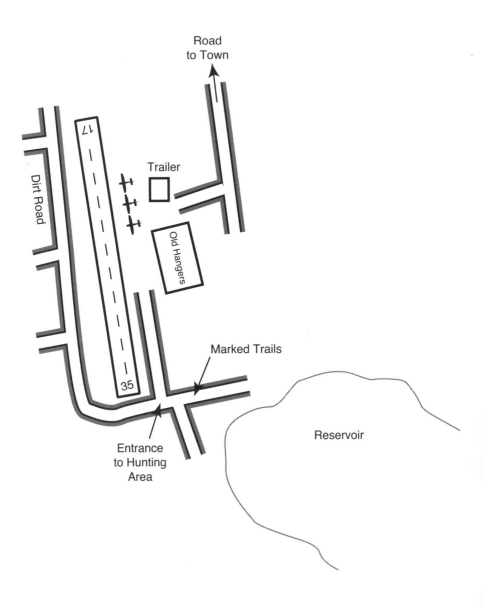

Tishomingo hunting area.

transportation. Signs for hunting, regulations, and seasons are posted at the end of runway 35. When I visited Tishomingo Airpark, I brought my mountain bike. Riding through the woods in the off-season, I saw deer and snakes. I have grown to recognize the zeal that Texans and other people of this region exhibit for a good hunt; therefore, I thought that this particular advantage—hunting within walking distance of the tie-down—is unique and attractive. Not being a hunter, I'm not sure how this area rates with respect to other hot spots of the Southwest; nevertheless, it seemed worth exploring. I did venture out around the area, a 5-mile radius, and found the surroundings to be quite pleasant and peaceful, a nice place for a day trip.

In this small and quiet Oklahoma town, there is the sense that you are traveling back in time at least 20 years. I remember the scene at the local IGA grocery store, a young man in an apron helping a woman with her bags to the car. You must admit in today's world of massive supermarkets open 24 hours a day, this is a bit unusual. There is little here to do and see outside of the nature preserve and the possibilities of hunting and mountain biking. In town, approximately 2 miles from the airfield, there is a Sonic Burger stand, convenient store, and grocery store. You will pass Murray State College on your way there.

When You Go:

Pack up your hunting gear and choose an autumn day for Tishomingo. (See the map for details of access to the hunting area.) If you like, bring some bicycles to ride into town. Don't count on any ground transportation or even interaction with the airport caretaker.

Contacts:

State of Oklahoma Department of Fisheries and Wildlife	(877) 532-0099
Tishomingo Airpark	(580) 371-2369

NEW MEXICO

Ski trails leading to the base of Angelfire resort.

Angelfire, New Mexico (AXX)

Location: Angelfire is a small community in the northeast corner of New Mexico, nestled in the Sangre de Cristo Mountains.

Airfield: The 10,000-foot strip at Angelfire is oriented north–south. Most pilots prefer to take off and land in a southerly direction. The 2-degree downgrade coupled with a field elevation of 8,300 feet favors takeoff and landings in this direction unless a considerable tailwind prevails. The strip surface is in excellent condition, sufficiently wide without obstruction at either end. There should be no misunderstanding, however; this is true mountain flying and the usual precautions associated with mountainous terrain and density altitude should be taken. There is no instrument approach here and that should be a hint of caution in and of itself. The authorities do not want to be responsible for vectoring airplanes in this region. Nevertheless, Angelfire is a wonderful place to visit in fair weather and light to moderate winds, and a well-planned trip here should not be discouraged.

Attractions:
Camping, horseback riding, hiking, mountain biking, stream/lake fishing, skiing, golf

Description: Angelfire is a small town located in a valley, surrounded by 12,000- to 13,000-foot mountains. It is a community of 3,000 year-round residents, and a quiet and favorite spot for vacationers with a particular love for the outdoors. Although there is some sense of community here, tourism is clearly the town's drawing card.

The Angelfire Resort is at the base of a ski area that caters to families and intermediate-level skiers. The resort is not far from the airport but there is really no center of town. A few shops and clusters of buildings represent the entire business community. There are no fancy restaurants or art galleries here, only wonderful scenery, mountains, lakes, and streams. Angelfire is one of the stops at the Enchanted Circle, a region of northern New Mexico, which is defined by a ring of 40 miles in circumference through high desert and mountainous terrain. Many folks drive the ring in a few days, stopping at the four or five towns along the way. The Angelfire Chamber of Commerce, a 2-minute drive from the airport is an excellent source of information and assistance.

When You Go:

Plan a summer trip to Angelfire and rent a car right from the airport. Be sure to prearrange this because there are only a couple of possibilities. Drive the Enchanted Circle if you wish or stay in Angelfire and visit a few of the day hiking or camping areas in the Kit Carson National Forest. Take a horseback ride from the riding stable, which is less than a mile from the airport. If you're feeling really athletic and have the lung capacity, try mountain biking at 8,300 feet. You can rent state-of-the-art bicycles from the cycle shop just across Route 434 from the airport entrance, 2 miles south. There are trails adjacent to the cycle shop. The Rocky Mountain Barbecue has a terrific chopped beef sandwich for lunch or dinner. This roadside restaurant has an outdoor patio and is located south of the airport on the main road, Route 434.

You can rent a boat for some lake fishing on Eagle's Nest Lake, approximately 8 miles to the north. Perhaps the prettiest stream in the area is the Cimarron River, which begins just north of Eagle's Nest joining the lake. Several camping areas along the stream are quite beautiful, and the trout fishing is excellent. Beware of the black bears that frequent these grounds, and be sure to keep your food in the car!

Contacts:

Angelfire Airport	(505) 377-3171
FBO, (Ross Aviation), Car Rental	(505) 377-3160
Angelfire Chamber of Commerce	(505) 377-6661;
	(800) 446-8117
Angelfire Resort	(505) 377-6401;
	(800) 633-7463
Bicycle Shop in Angelfire—	
Mountain Sports	(505) 377-6803
Angelfire Stables (Horseback Riding)	(505) 377-3828
Local taxi	(505) 377-6856

Las Vegas, New Mexico (LVS)

Location: On the eastern plains of New Mexico. The area is just on the eastern slope of a range of 10,000- to 11,000-foot mountains.

Airfield: Las Vegas Municipal Airport, in the high desert plains, has an elevation of 6,900 feet and the longest of two runways measures 8,200 feet by 60 feet. There is nothing difficult about landing here if you are familiar with mountain flying and the hazardous conditions that winds and weather can generate in this environment.

   The airport facilities are typical for a municipal airport that gets very little use. A loaner car is available at the airport, but beware—it was in marginal mechanical condition when I used it. The airfield sits 5 miles from the central city of Las Vegas. If you are staying at the Plaza Hotel, shuttle service is available. Otherwise, try Meadow City Cab, or a rental car from the local Ford dealership can be prearranged.

Attractions:

   Hiking/climbing, sight-seeing (historical landmarks of the Old West), Native American culture, camping, Santa Fe Trail, Armand Hammer United World College

Description: Las Vegas, New Mexico, is situated along the Santa Fe Trail. This route is a well-defined path that was used by settlers, explorers, traders, and cattlemen as they traveled from cities like Kansas City, Missouri, to the Far West, across the Rocky Mountains. Traveling east to west, Santa Fe was the first major stop or commercial center after approximately 900 miles of trail through the eastern plains from Missouri. Las Vegas is approximately 60 miles to the east of Santa Fe. Many interesting facts about the Santa Fe Trail and the significance of Las Vegas as a crossroads in American western culture are described by nearly all guides to the region.

   For me, Las Vegas is reminiscent of the Wild West. The architecture, topography, and general ambience all combine to create this feeling of the Old West. The largest hotel in town, the Plaza, is decorated as an establishment one would typically see in a western movie, complete with saloon. There are a few other restaurants in town within walking distance, which feature hearty fare, steaks, and southwestern cuisine.

   There is not much shopping in town, but a few points of historical interest are notable. The general area surrounding Las Vegas is particularly scenic, especially the Pecos Wilderness, a series of canyons and ranges to the west. Hiking here is quite beautiful and a variety of trails for the serious backpacker as well as for the casual day-tripper can be accessed. There are several hot springs, which provide a soothing and some believe medicinal benefit. The Armand Hammer United World College is located just out of town to the west. This is a uniquely progressive college that has gained national acclaim. It's worth a visit if you are interested in environmental issues or the performing arts, particular strengths of this community.

When You Go:

Fly to Las Vegas, New Mexico, in the morning. The afternoon buildups can culminate in significant thunderstorm activity. For some reason, the area is particularly prone to this type of weather pattern during the summer. Stay at the Plaza Hotel and take a brief walk around town, soaking up the flavor and ambience of the Wild West. Have dinner at El Rialto, the steak place down the street from the Plaza. Plan a day trip to the Pecos Wilderness via the Guyanes Canyon. Even if you don't opt for a vigorous hike, the drive through the canyon is magnificent. There are beautiful trees and meadows, a lovely pastoral setting. On your way back, stop at the hot springs just outside of the entrance to the university. Las Vegas, New Mexico, is a place to really slow down and smell the cactus. Be sure to leave your cell phone at home!

Contacts:

Las Vegas Municipal Airport	(505) 454-0881
Plaza Hotel	(505) 425-3591;
	(800) 328-1882
Armand Hammer United World College	(505) 454-4200
Meadow City Cab	(505) 454-1864
Highlands Ford (car rental)	(505) 425-7545
Las Vegas Chamber of Commerce	(800) 832-5947

Questa, New Mexico (N24)

Location: Northwest corner of New Mexico within the Enchanted Circle

Airfield: Questa Municipal Airport is nothing more than a 6,800-foot paved strip with pilot-controlled lights in mountainous terrain. This is strictly a VFR airport, but with fairly open approaches on either end of the north–south runway. There are no airport services and ground transportation is particularly difficult. The nearest convenience store is more than a few miles away and the town of Questa, which is no thriving metropolis, is 6 miles to the south.

Attractions:
Camping, hiking, touring the Enchanted Circle

Description: Questa Municipal Airport is included in this guide as a gateway to a very beautiful and secluded park. The strip is located just north of a turn-off to the west that takes you to the Wild Rivers Recreational Area. This state and national preservation occupies several miles of land next to the Rio Grande. A steep canyon with dramatic and rugged cliffs lines this river, which travels through four states. The Rio Grande is picturesque and dramatic at this point, and there are several camping areas along this stretch of river. In addition, easy day hikes and picnic areas are accessible from the main drive. Even during the high tourist season, there are never crowds, and you can always find privacy, seclusion, and serenity.

The problem with traveling to this area is ground transportation. My suggestion is to prearrange this with the car dealership or rental agency in Red River. Alternatively, if you are equipped with a motorized vehicle or bicycles, this would be ideal. The need for self-sufficiency is essential, however, and the complete camping experience is emphasized. The only shelters in the park are a few scattered lean-tos along the Rio Grande. River activities include rafting, kayaking, fishing, and swimming. Most of the year the water is extremely cool and the source of mountain runoff.

The local people are typically a combination of Spanish and Native American. They are friendly and accommodating and their communities are small, simple, and quiet. There is no industry here and the town of Questa is nothing more than a post office and a few other businesses—that is, grocery store, hardware store, restaurant, and motel.

Questa (N24)

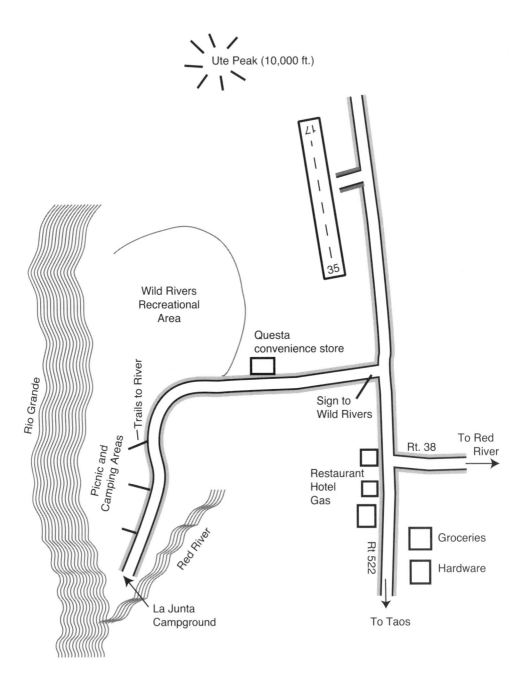

Ute Peak (10,000 ft.)

17

35

Wild Rivers
Recreational
Area

Questa
convenience store

Trails to River

Sign to
Wild Rivers

Rio Grande

To Red
River

Rt. 38

Picnic and
Camping Areas

Restaurant
Hotel
Gas

Groceries

Hardware

Rt 522

Red River

La Junta
Campground

To Taos

Camping grounds along the Rio Grande, Questa, New Mexico.

Ten miles to the east is Red River, a larger town and more reminiscent of the Old West. There is a ski area at Red River, less well known than Taos to the south, but it is more family oriented with lower elevation and easier trails. Horseback riding and fishing are popular summer activities to arrange out of Red River. More shops, restaurants, and hotels are found here. Both Red River and Questa are destinations along a ring of towns that occupy this region known as the Enchanted Circle.

The consequence of an elk hunt, near Questa, New Mexico.

To drive this 60-mile circumference nonstop would take approximately 3 hours but most people do it in a span of 2 or 3 days, stopping at each small town along the way.

When You Go:

Travel to Questa and visit the Wild Rivers Recreational Area. The last stop, deep within the park, is La Junta. This is the convergence of the Rio Grande and the Red River and is a particularly beautiful spot to spend an afternoon or even overnight. Bring your fishing rod, swimsuit, and camping gear. There are small, well-camouflaged huts along the riverbank where you can find shelter. There are no other accommodations, like running water, electricity, and heat. Alternatively, you can take a trip into Red River and walk the main street, stopping at the various shops and souvenir stores. You can arrange for horseback riding or day-hike in this beautiful mountainous setting.

Contacts:

Questa Municipal Airport	(505) 586-0694
Red River Chamber of Commerce	(505) 754-2366;
	(800) 348-6444

Ruidoso, New Mexico/Sierra Blanca Airport (SRR)

Location: South-central New Mexico, mountainous terrain

Airfield: The general aviation gateway to Ruidoso, New Mexico, is Sierra Blanca Airport, which consists of two intersecting runways just east of a range of 12,000-foot mountains. The longest of two runway surfaces is 8,000 feet, and it is wide, smooth, and well maintained. The main concerns at Sierra Blanca are mountain waves, wind shear, and strong crosswinds. An intersecting runway was recently constructed here for just this reason. Exercise extreme caution on a gusty day, especially in high-wing light aircraft. If you are unfamiliar with crosswind landing technique, this is a good place to practice it in moderate to light winds.

Sierra Blanca Airport is attended 24 hours a day. For an uncontrolled airport that gets very little use, especially in the wintertime, this field

The high desert environment of Riudoso, New Mexico, Sierra Blanca Airport.

Riudoso airport terminal area and a backdrop of mountains.

is "full service." The FBO attendants are extremely helpful and courteous. They will provide you with a wealth of information about the surrounding area, a rental car, and so on. You can choose an outside tie-down for a minimal overnight fee; sunshade is $20 a night and hangar space, when available, is $35.

Attractions:
Skiing, equestrian, cultural events

Description: Ruidoso is known for a few special recreational activities. A ski area is situated approximately 15 miles from the airfield. There are also a number of equestrian activities. Among these, horseback-riding tours, as well as horse racing, are popular. As you leave the airport and head toward town, just before you reach Route 48, you'll see a modern building with unique geometric design. This is the Spencer Theatre, which hosts concerts and performances during weekends. The acoustics are fantastic and most events are well worth attending.

As you approach town from the north on Route 48, the road changes to Mechem Drive and then to Sudderth. Most of the businesses, shops, and restaurants line this roadway. A nice place to stop for a sandwich or lunch on your way in is Farley's, on the east side of the road. The center of town is inundated with craft shops, gift shops, and ski shops. If you are looking for a quiet dinner, La Lorraine is your best bet. The food is fine French cuisine and the atmosphere is elegant.

Accommodations in Ruidoso are numerous and available in a variety of price ranges. The Inn of the Mountain Gods is perhaps the best-known resort. This is only a few miles from the center of town off Carrizo Road. The resort sits on a large parcel of land and has its own casino, riding stables, golf course, and small lake. It is quite scenic here and, as suggested, everything is right at your fingertips.

When You Go:

Choose a summer day or nice weekend to visit Ruidoso. Study the VFR chart well and know your wind conditions around the time of arrival. Arrange for a rental car from the FBO and a room at the Inn of the Mountain Gods and ask to prearrange for a sunset horseback ride from its on-site stables. After dinner, try not to lose too much in the casino so you can enjoy the rest of your stay! Call ahead to the Spencer Theatre and inquire about its weekend show or concert schedule.

Contacts:

Sierra Blanca Airport	(505) 336-8111
Inn of the Mountain Gods	(800) 545-9011;
	(505) 257-5141
Spencer Theatre	(888) 818-7872
Equibest Equestrian Center	(505) 336-7090

Santa Fe, New Mexico (SAF)

Location: Santa Fe Municipal Airport just south and west of the Sangre de Cristo mountains in north-central New Mexico in mountainous terrain.

Airfield: The airport at Santa Fe is a controlled field with three intersecting runways, the longest measuring 8,300 feet. There is very little commercial activity here and only a few small carriers service the field. Use is geared mainly to private general aviation aircraft and corporate jets. Most of the time, airport activity and traffic are relatively low and approach control will accommodate you for practice approaches on the various runways.

The city itself has become increasingly popular and during certain weekends and festival times stress level and volume of airport traffic flow are heightened. ILS, GPS, and VOR approaches are available. Although the field is a distance from major peaks, mountain waves and wind shear off this high plains environment should be a consideration. The FBO at the field, Santa Fe Jet Center, has excellent service including catering, rental cars, and help with accommodations. Overnight hangars and tie-downs are also available. The 6,000-foot field elevation mandates you be familiar with the concept of density altitude during the summer.

Attractions:
    Southwestern art, hiking, biking, Santa Fe opera, various other performing arts, horseback riding

Description: Santa Fe is hardly off the beaten path as a destination. It is a great place for a long weekend, however, and access to the general aviation pilot makes it a must for this guide. If you haven't been here in a while, you may be surprised at the recent changes it has undergone since its image of a quiet western town in the 1970s or '80s. It has become the epicenter of southwestern art, earning international acclaim, and is the home of a world-famous opera company. This has influenced and help build a reputation in other performing arts, such as symphony and chamber music and dance. Still, this region has retained a rich tradition in Native American culture and folklore, and has a Spanish influence as well.

    Santa Fe is also a place where people come to enjoy a spa-type experience with emphasis on health, spirituality, and stress relief. This is not to say that the atmosphere is entirely basic or primitive. The level of sophistication in food, art, and music is typical of a very cosmopolitan area.

The opera at Santa Fe is a unique experience. This outdoor, partially covered amphitheater has earned its renown in recent years. Performances occur frequently in July and August throughout the week.

Prices in Santa Fe are higher than in most other cities of New Mexico and this applies to accommodations, restaurants, and upscale shopping. As mentioned, the focus on southwestern art is unmistakable here and many people come to purchase art from the galleries that have infiltrated the town. Canyon Road has the highest concentration of galleries in the area. The city is centered on the plaza, a rectangular array of buildings that are a mix of New Mexican, Native American, and Spanish traditions. Although Santa Fe has a few restaurants and hotels with New York City prices, don't be scared off—it is a simple matter to access the natural splendor of this region just outside the city limits. Many beautiful hiking trails and bike paths are easily accessible, within a 10- to 20-minute drive. Though the summertime is by far the high season for Santa Fe, winter activities are possible as well. Santa Fe has its own ski area and the town is beautifully decorated for the Christmas holidays.

When You Go:

It is difficult to recommend a time to visit Santa Fe; with few exceptions, you can't go wrong. Perhaps my favorite is late June. My suggestions on accommodations are highly dependent on the experience you want to have. The elegant Inn of the Anasazi is a wonderful place to stay and its restaurant is among the finest in Santa Fe. A number of nice bed-and-breakfasts offer a more private environment than that of the Inn, which is adjacent to the plaza. A favorite restaurant is La Sena, where the food is matched to the atmosphere, both A+. Plan ahead, reserve opera tickets, and be prepared for an all-night affair. The show usually starts at nine and ends around midnight.

If you're in the mood for self-indulgence, then Ten Thousand Waves is an experience you may not want to pass up. This spa is highly recommended by those who have stayed there and partaken of the massages, baths, and aromatherapy for which it is best known.

A simple walk around town is a good idea as well. After having been to Santa Fe several times, I took a guided walking tour and wished I had done this previously. The experience was wonderfully informative and equally entertaining. Along one side of the plaza, Native American craftsmen will be peddling their handicrafts. These artifacts are worth browsing, as are some of the more elegant boutiques in town. Keep control of your charge cards if you can!

As suggested, the area is rich in natural beauty and a mecca for the outdoorsman. There are so many activities that to list them would be exhaustive. Please see recommendations below for a few ideas. Santa Fe is a true gem of the Southwest, and worth at least one long weekend.

Contacts:

Santa Fe Municipal Airport	(505) 473-7243
Inn of the Anasazi	(505)988-3030;
	(800) 688-8100
Eldorado Hotel	(800) 955-4455;
	(505) 988-4455
Ten Thousand Waves	(505) 982-9304;
	(505) 992-5025
Radisson Santa Fe	(800) 333-3750;
	(505) 992-5800
Santa Fe Opera	(505) 986-5955;
	(800) 280-4654
Santa Fe Rafting Company	(800) 467-RAFT
Georgia O'Keeffe Museum	(505) 946-1000

Taos, New Mexico (SKX)

Location: Just west of the Sangre de Cristo Mountains, a range of 13,000-foot peaks in northern New Mexico

Airfield: Taos Municipal Airport, with its field elevation of 7,000 feet and runway length of 6,000 feet, should be approached with confidence but also caution. Extreme caution should always be exercised when flying in proximity to mountains of this magnitude. Respect density altitude, especially during the summer. That said, this airfield is strategically placed within an expansive, open, high plains area. It is essential to study the VFR chart prior to your approach. Most pilots prefer to use runway 22 if the winds are light and variable or favoring this runway. There is a slight downslope in the direction of 22 and the power lines just before the threshold would be potential hazards for a missed approach in the opposite direction. I have landed from both directions, and neither presents a considerable hazard. The VOR approach is an option into Taos, but I think that the concept of personal minimums, especially in mountainous terrain, should be the rule of thumb here.

I flew the VOR approach into Taos under the hood with my instructor and it was a very valuable experience. On a spectacularly clear day, from 12,000 to 10,000 feet, there was moderate turbulence and for me this created a particular challenge in controlling the aircraft. I would not be enthusiastic about landing at this airport as the ceilings approach minimums. I'm told that approach control doesn't want the responsibility of orchestrating vectors to a precision approach, and that's why there's none at airports like Taos. I can understand this after flying the practice approach. In any case, there is nothing to fear in moderate winds and good visibility.

The airport has undergone considerable renovation. The strip was widened and resurfaced, more hangar space was added, and a new FBO is in place as of October 1999. Rental cars are available, if prearranged, and the attendants are extremely helpful. One commercial airline, Rio Grande Airways, flies in and out of Taos to Santa Fe, Albuquerque, and Los Alamos. The folks at the FBO will hangar your plane and/or facilitate cold starts, as requested.

Attractions:

Horseback riding, fishing, on- and off-road cycling, camping, hiking, Southwestern art, Native American culture, rafting

Sunrise at Taos, New Mexico.

Description: One of the oldest communities in New Mexico, Taos is rich in Southwestern and Native American culture and art. There is enough to do here for a lifetime, so probably one weekend will not be sufficient. Aside from Native Americans, most of the people who live here are transplants who have opted out of the rat race of big-city life. The community attracts free-spirited people, and this is noticeable after being there just a short while. The natural resources at Taos are well known and the Taos Ski Valley has earned international acclaim as one of the most challenging in the western United States. In a way, Taos is a melting pot for a spectrum of individuals, from intellectuals to hippies, from artists to leaders of the Native American Cultural Society. Direct descendants of some of the first Spanish settlers have a strong presence here as well. This makes for a very interesting community of people with interests aside from tourism.

The air most days is cool and crisp and the sky is as blue as I have ever seen. The Rio Grande winds its way through the high plains to the west of the city, creating a spectacular gorge 800 feet deep and the

Williams Lake, a popular hiking destination, mid-September, Taos Ski Valley.

wonderful opportunity for white-water activities like rafting, tubing, kayaking, and fly fishing. The Taos Pueblo is worth a visit, especially if you have never been to a pueblo before.

Accommodations in Taos vary in price and comfort level and are readily available most times of the year. Expect to pay a lot more during peak ski season and during special weekends, such as the arts, film, and balloon festivals.

When You Go:

I've spent quite a bit of time in Taos and have visited there during all seasons. My favorite time of year here is summer. Because of its elevation, you will never experience oppressive heat. A rafting expedition of half a day in "the box" is a nice way to start your vacation. A climb up to Williams Lake, nestled among the 13,000-foot peaks at Taos Ski Valley, is another wonderful half-day adventure. Fly-fishing guides are available to show you some of the more beautiful rivers and streams in the area, and can provide you with the best opportunity for landing trout.

Mountain biking at altitude is quite difficult and an activity only for the well-trained off-road cyclist who is acclimatized. There is a beautiful trail that courses along the edge of the Rio Grande gorge just after you cross the bridge on the west side. This west-rim trail is flat with few technical hazards—perfect for the beginner to intermediate rider. It is a shared hiking and biking path with great views. The vast expanse in front of you, with the backdrop of 14,000-foot mountains, is a therapeutic panorama. If you are less of an outdoor sportsman and prefer to spend the afternoon browsing art galleries or shops, Taos is a wonderful place to do that as well. There is a Nambé Factory Outlet just north of the plaza on the main road through town on the west side. The plaza has many stores with novelties and souvenirs made by people from this region. Taos has excellent restaurants with every different type of atmosphere and cuisine available (see listing below).

Contacts:

Taos Municipal Airport and FBO	(505) 758-4995
Accommodations in Taos	
Best Western Kachina Lodge	(505) 758-2275;
	(800) 522-4462
Taos Inn	(505) 758-2233;
	(888) 518-8267
Accommodations out of town	
Ski Valley: The Bavarian	(505) 776-8020
Adobe and Stars, Bed and Breakfast	(800) 211-7076;
	(505) 776-2776
The Taos Inn	(800) TAOS-INN;
	(505) 758-2233
Rafting	
Los Rios River Runners	(505) 776-8854;
	(800) 544-1181
Far Flung Adventures	(505) 758-2628
Gearing Up Bicycle Shop	(505) 751-0365
Restaurants	
Trading Post Café	(505) 758-5089
Joseph's Table	(505) 751-4512
Apple Tree Restaurant	(505) 758-1900

TEXAS

Addison Airport, gateway to Dallas.

Addison, Texas (ADS)

Location: North Dallas, within the metroplex area

Airfield: Addison Airport is an extremely high-use airfield serving the metroplex area, specifically Dallas. This single-strip, 7,200 feet long, is oriented north–south and is shared by general aviation pilots with a high volume of corporate aircraft, including jets. I was told that this airport is the second busiest noncommercial airport in the country. A special caution to any pilot who wishes to attempt an approach to runway 33 in low IFR conditions: Beware! The approach to 33 is quite close to a number of large buildings comprising a commercial financial district. It would be quite unnerving for the inexperienced pilot to fly in here at peak-use times and under serious instrument conditions.

Nevertheless, Addison is the closest municipal airfield to Dallas proper, and the most convenient. Abundant services around the airport make this a popular destination point as well. Several FBOs, repair shops, special services, and restaurants along with two pilot shops, can be accessed by Addison. Many of these services offer ground transportation.

Attractions:

Flight museum, shopping, dining

Description: Addison is listed in this guide as a gateway to Dallas, but also for those aviation buffs who would enjoy the flight museum here. The Cavanaugh Flight Museum is situated at the north end of the field and features mostly military aircraft war birds, from historic World War I planes to recent high-tech jet fighters. The exhibition is housed in four hangars within walking distance of most FBOs. Guided tours are available if prearranged for small groups, but this is not necessary if you are only a few people. Museum hours are 9 to 5 daily.

At the south end of the airport, along Addison Road, are two excellent restaurants. The first is Sambucca, an eclectic establishment featuring Mediterranean cuisine and often hosting live music, particularly jazz. A few doors down is Texas de Brazil, a Brazilian steakhouse that is a unique dining experience. It's an all-you-can-eat extravaganza for the die-hard carnivore. Another famous steakhouse just around the corner from the airport, less than 2 miles away, is Del Frisco's. This establishment is expensive but quite popular among beef connoisseurs. Less than 1 mile south of the airport is Beltline Road, which is also known as restaurant row. There is virtually every type of food along here and the atmosphere ranges from casual to sophisticated. If you are looking for easy access to Dallas, education in aviation history, or a satisfying and cholesterol-laden dining experience, then Addison is your destination.

When You Go:

Plan a trip to Addison at a non-peak-use time. Stop off at the flight museum, then head to the Galleria for a shopping spree by cab or loaner car. Have dinner on your way back at one of the restaurants suggested for a true taste of North Dallas.

Contacts:

Addison Airport	(972) 248-7733
Mercury Air Center (FBO)	(972) 930-0216
Monarch Air (closest FBO to the flight museum)	(972) 931-0345
Hertz Rent-A-Car at Addison Airport	(972) 680-0224
Cavanaugh Flight Museum	(972) 380-8800
Sambucca Jazz Café	(972) 385-8455
Hot Shots Sports Grill (on field)	(972) 713-0000
Texas de Brazil	(972) 385-1000

Corpus Christi, Texas (CRP)

Location: South Texas, on the Gulf Coast

Airfield: Corpus Christi International Airport is your typical large, yet small, airport. The field caters to general aviation as well as commercial activity, but there is nothing to fear about getting in and out of this place. It is sleepy most times, especially on weekends. Two intersecting runways, the longer one 6,750 feet long, make landing here a breeze and, with no pun intended, that is your only precaution. The approach areas are wide, flat, and easy to pick out from a distance, and the only considerable hazard is gusty wind shear on final.

A variety of services are available once you land. These include all major rental car agencies along with shuttles to hotels. Signature Flight Support FBO is north of the tower and particularly convenient. These folks arranged a rental car for me and provided superb hospitality, and there was no overnight parking fee!

Attractions:

Gulf-side events, Corpus Christi boardwalk, the aquarium, the U.S.S. *Lexington* Museum

Description: Corpus Christi is a well-known Gulf-side metropolis, which I have included really for one purpose. The U.S.S. *Lexington* is an aircraft carrier that resides just to the north of the city. This ship has been there since 1991, after it was decommissioned. This floating museum was, for me, an opportunity to see a piece of America's history and my first chance at boarding an aircraft carrier. The museum is quite user friendly, with wheelchair accessibility, and worth at least an hour or two of exploration. Several aircraft occupy the top (flight) deck. A range of fighters and reconnaissance planes or jets are accompanied by written placard explanations or a guided tour, if you prefer. The hangar deck just below houses more planes, many of which are of great historical significance. You can ascend to the flying bridge of the ship to see the captain's quarters and the controls. Other interesting points and areas of this ship are easily accessible. These include a flight simulator as well as the engine room. Finally, the ship/museum includes an I-MAX theater. Usually two shows are alternating throughout the daylight hours. The theater is large, comfortable, and a great place to relax and take in the surround-sound entertainment.

The U.S.S. Lexington, floating museum, Corpus Christi, Texas.

Corpus Christi has a wonderful aquarium not far from the museum. Access and parking are clearly marked and simple. The city of Corpus Christi is, I'm sorry to say, rather uninteresting. The drive from the airport will overemphasize its industrial roots. Like many other Gulf-side communities, the oil industry is the driving force, and it is visually dominating. As you drive toward the main shoreline avenue, all you will see is oil tanks and heavy construction equipment.

When you get to Shoreline Drive, however, you will be forced to turn either left or right along a wonderful promenade. This is a great boardwalk to cycle, walk, or in-line skate for a couple of hours. There are no crowds and the atmosphere is pure relaxation. You will see young families, fishermen, and a few vendors, but mostly just water and whitecaps with sailboats and fishing boats in the distance. Along this boardwalk stretch are several major hotels that offer very reasonable rates. Back from Shoreline Drive, accommodations are even less expensive.

The city has an unmistakable Hispanic influence and the atmosphere is purely one of slow pace, serenity, and seafood! Dining in Corpus

Christi is neither elegant nor pricey. Numerous waterside or dockside establishments are easily visible from the promenade.

North Padre Island begins just across the bridge from Corpus Christi. If you are looking for a beach experience with less industry, more seclusion, waterfowl, and nicer swimming areas, then head this way.

This uncontrolled airport is ideal for a day trip to the beach. Beware, there is no fuel at Mustang Island. See "Mustang Island (2R8)" for more information.

When You Go:

The author on the flight deck of the U.S.S. Lexington.

Take a group of aviation enthusiasts to Corpus Christi and visit the U.S.S. *Lexington.* Combine your trip with a stop at the aquarium or a promenade along Shoreline Drive. The aquarium is easy to access from the major hotels along Shoreline Drive, but the aircraft carrier will require either a taxi or a rental car. Visit North Padre Island for a half a day, or take a fishing trip or sight-seeing boat tour out of Corpus Christi. Sit by the Gulf at a restaurant or bring a picnic to one of the hundreds of benches or gazebos that line the boardwalk. Most of all, enjoy the seafood and slow pace.

Contacts:

Corpus Christi International Airport	(361) 289-0171
Signature Flight Support FBO	(512) 289-0585
U.S.S. *Lexington* Museum	(512) 888-4873
Omni Bayfront Hotel	(512) 882-1700
Water Street Seafood Company	(512) 882-8684
Sand Dollar Hospitality B&B Reservation Service	(800) 528-7782

Galveston, Texas/Scholes Field (GLS)

Location: Southeast of Houston on the Gulf Coast

Airfield: Scholes Field is a municipal airport, 2 miles from the center of Galveston and about 2 miles from the water. Very little commercial activity takes place here, and the airport is relatively quiet for its size and the number of services available. The approach is wide open with three intersecting, long, smooth, wide runways. This is an excellent place to practice approaches and landings.

Rental cars are available from the FBO at Scholes Field, and with the exception of extremely busy times, reservations are not required. The only real challenge in flying to Galveston comes with ATC communications in Houston class B airspace. Be prepared during "heavy-use" times, and avoid penetrating class B is the best advice I can offer.

Attractions:

Beach activities, bicycling the promenade, shopping, historical downtown

Description: Galveston, a moderate-sized city for Texas, has neither the prettiest coastline nor the clearest water along the Gulf of Mexico, but it's a great weekend getaway. The beachfront is commercial and often crowded, but its easy access and lively atmosphere make it at least a one-time must. Options for boating, fishing, and sailing are numerous here, and right at your fingertips. Most of the accommodations line the main road, which runs parallel to the beach. There are a few fine hotels and condominiums along this boardwalk, as well as many affordable less elegant motels (see Contacts). One of my favorite activities in Galveston is to take a bicycle or a pair of in-line skates and travel the boardwalk. This is a great thing to do when humidity and heat permit. Often these factors are kept in check by a stiff sea breeze. The people watching, too, is excellent.

As mentioned above, accommodations in Galveston range from motels to elegant surf-side condominiums. The Hotel Galvez is a favorite of mine. This reconditioned beachside hotel has spectacular water views and interesting architecture. The pool is often a hotbed of activity with poolside live music during the busy season. The hotel has undergone substantial renovations over the past few years. If you are familiar with its previous state, you may be pleasantly surprised at the recent upgrades. Its central location and new facade make it worth revisiting. If you are looking for a condominium or quieter atmosphere, several possibilities exist. There are some bed-and-breakfasts in the area that offer a more private, quiet, and romantic alternative.

Galveston is one of the oldest ports along the Gulf Coast. The downtown harbor is well worth a visit. The history and architecture within these few blocks are easily explored by foot. In addition, there is an atmosphere of sophistication, progressive lifestyle, and academic importance here, as Galveston has the reputation of being somewhat of a college town. A few surrounding streets are lined with Victorian homes that are more typical of those one would see in South Carolina or even in New England. This makes for an interesting walk or short diversion before or after lunch at one of the great restaurants in the old port district.

When You Go:

Plan a weekend when the humidity is predictably low (spring/fall), unless you are used to it. Visit the downtown area for dinner one night and try one of the Gulf-side establishments on the boardwalk for lunch or cocktails as well. Rent a bicycle or in-line skates and go out to the boardwalk in the morning or evening. Or just relax and eat some world-famous seafood.

Contacts:

Galveston Scholes Field Airport	(409) 744-1606
Gulf Coast Jet Center (FBO)	(409) 740-1223
Galveston Convention and Visitors Bureau	(800) 351-4236
Hotel Galvez	(409) 765-7721
Willie G's (seafood restaurant by the harbor)	(409) 762-3030
Saltwater Grill Restaurant	(409) 762-3474

Horseshoe Bay, Texas (Private)

Location: Horseshoe Bay is an inlet off the southern tip of Lake LBJ, 30 miles west of Austin in the hill country.

Airfield: Although the airfield at Horseshoe Bay is private, permission to land there for general aviation aircraft is granted virtually automatically. People at the field office are friendly, helpful, and accommodating. A shuttle service between the main resort at Horseshoe Bay and the airfield is efficient and really first-rate with roomy new air-conditioned vans. The 6,000-foot runway is smooth-surfaced and extremely well maintained, and the visual approach is clear and simple at either end. Runway 17 guides you in over the lake and is usually favored with the prevailing breeze.

Plush facilities at the airfield office, phones, lounge with TV and other amenities, make it an ideal place to do some preflight planning. Rental cars are available from the airfield if prearranged. The folks at the airfield will call the shuttle for you, a 5-minute-ride to the resort, if this is your destination.

Attractions:

Golf, lakeside water sports, spa with massage, tennis, horseback riding

Description: Horseshoe Bay is an upscale lakeside air park community on Lake LBJ, northwest of Austin. The hill country is quite beautiful, and if you have never been here, it is definitely worth exploring. The air park community is surrounded by tastefully zoned and well-constructed homes. Proximity of the lots to the airstrip requires noise abatement procedures and restricted use. This 6,000-foot runway is commonly shared by corporate jets and GA light aircraft and is meticulously maintained.

At the resort, 2 miles away, there is an air of elitism and luxury compared to some of the other Texas lakeside communities. The prices for accommodations are rather steep, especially during the high season. However, you get what you pay for, as the saying goes, and the ambience is quite elegant, the facilities are new, and the service is excellent. The resort caters to a somewhat older and more conservative clientele— more golfers and fewer bass fishermen! During the regular season there are three restaurants and three excellent golf courses. Golf packages are

The airpark community of Horseshoe Bay as seen from the south.

available. Other resort activities can be arranged with a little bit of planning. The resort management is very helpful and informative.

The resort offers a variety of accommodation options. You can rent anything from a large and comfortable condominium to a more basic hotel room. You can be as close to the water as you like, with a porch that looks out onto Lake LBJ, or at a more inland location, depending on your preference and room availability. I visited Horseshoe Bay during the high season and was surprised how quiet it was despite the fact that almost all of the rooms were occupied. Dining room options at the resort are available most of the year, ranging from casual to elegant, and the marina at Horseshoe Bay offers a wide variety of watercraft and water sport rentals for recreational activities on the lake.

When You Go:

Choose a spring or fall weekend to visit Horseshoe Bay. If you're not accustomed to Texas heat, you'll find the midsummer oppressive, even lakeside. Call ahead if you want to do some horseback riding or golfing and inquire about the golf packages (talk to the pros about which course would suit you best). Enjoy a relaxing weekend and consider a visit to the spa as well. The cost is $10 per day for guests of the resort. Most important, bring someone with whom you can share the experience and who will derive an equal amount of relaxation and pleasure from the self-pampering!

Contacts:

Horseshoe Bay Airpark	(830) 598-6386
Horseshoe Bay Resort	(800) 531-5105 (outside of Texas); (800) 252-9363 (within Texas)
Horseshoe Bay Marina	(830) 598-9401
Horseshoe Bay Golf	
Slickrock Proshop	(830) 598-2561
Captrock Proshop	(830) 598-6561
Enterprise Rental Car	(830) 693-8970

Jefferson, Texas/Cypress River (24F)

Location: East Texas, approximately 110 miles east of Dallas and just west of Tyler

Airfield: Cypress River Airfield is a small municipal paved strip 3,100 feet long. There are no services at the field, no telephone or restroom. The topographical landmarks are challenging to pick out, but the town of Jefferson is 3.1 miles to the west, perhaps your best landmark. The visual approach is not difficult, although the wooded area surrounding the field makes it imperative that you approach at a significant angle of attack at both ends of the runway. One thing for sure is that you won't encounter a lot of traffic in the pattern! In fact, in the several times I have been here, I have never even seen another plane land.

There is no fuel available, so be prepared. I use my foldable bikes to travel to town from the airfield. There are no hills along the route and the road leading to town is relatively quiet, with respect to traffic.

Attractions:

Antique shopping, river boat rides, horseback riding, pure and simple relaxation, bed-and-breakfasts, Caddo Lake

Description: Jefferson is a historical landmark town that is purely and typically east Texas. At one time, it was one of the largest and most commercially active cities in the state. The topography, atmosphere, and architecture seem more characteristic of Louisiana. There are bayous just adjacent to the airport area and the Cypress River courses right through this small town. Nevertheless, this is Texas, and the people of Jefferson are proud of their heritage, history, and association with the Lone Star State. There is a museum in town that emphasizes this.

On my initial trip to Jefferson, the first thing I noticed when I stepped out of the plane was the delicious smell of cypress trees. This was unmistakable and really refreshing.

Jefferson is popular for a weekend getaway with its many bed-and-breakfasts. Luxurious accommodations can be found year-round. A disproportionate number of antique shops target the discriminating shopper (less so, the bargain hunter). There are a few restaurants that seem to cater to the up scale weekend crowd as well, but the atmosphere is far from pretentious. Although Jefferson is well known as a romantic getaway, it is still quiet and unspoiled almost all the time. One

Jefferson (24F)

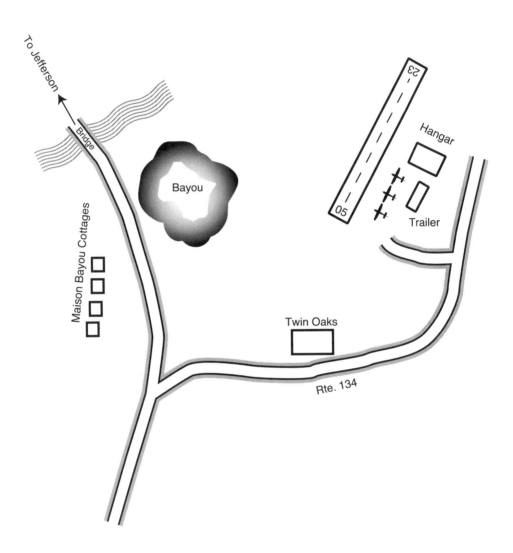

A riverboat tour is a great way to see the bayous and acquaint yourself with the history of Jefferson, Texas.

exception may be right before Christmas, when shoppers and traffic seem to make this small country town swell.

The Twin Oaks Country Inn is a Georgian mansion with large Doric columns at its main entrance. This B&B is located approximately half a mile from the airport on your right as you head to town on route 134N. The hosts will pick you up from the airport and provide you with the necessary transportation into town if you decide to stay with them. The grounds of their inn are quite beautiful and the southern hospitality is sure to make you want to come back. Farther toward town on your left there is a small group of cabins in the woods with private stables called the Maison Bayou. It is a different experience, rustic and less luxurious that caters more to families. It makes for a terrific getaway also.

The river that winds through town is lovely and connects with a few bayous. At certain times of the year, a riverboat cruise is fun, but during the oppressively humid months, this experience can be too

Foldable bikes are ideal for the 2-mile ride between Jefferson airport and town.

steamy. The most popular activities in Jefferson are just browsing around town, antiquing, and perhaps a brief trip to a small but unique museum that displays the town's historical archives.

Caddo Lake is one of the only natural lakes in Texas, 15 miles to the east of the airport. It has an excellent reputation for fishing and other recreational water sports. Lakeside accommodations are available as well. Transportation to this area is the main challenge. The airport in Marshall, Texas, Harrison County (ASL), has taxi and rental car services for the local area, and would be the preferred field of access.

When You Go:

Plan a weekend or overnight to Jefferson and call ahead at the Twin Oaks Country Inn. Ask your hosts to make dinner reservations for you and to arrange for transportation. Take a stroll through town or a riverboat cruise. Go for a horseback ride through the woods or just stop at a bayou, smell the cypress, and watch the day go by.

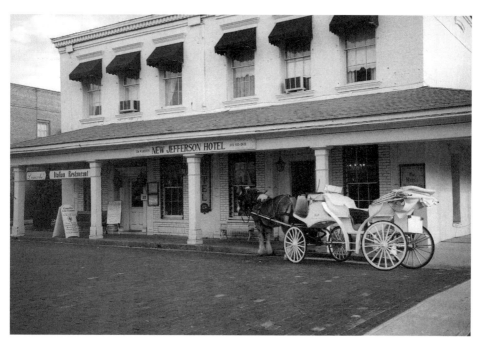

Jefferson, Texas: A town suspended in time.

Contacts:

Cypress River Airfield	(903) 665-3261
Jefferson Reservation Service	(877) 603-2535;
www.jeffersonreservationservice.com	
Chamber of Commerce	(888) GO-RELAX
Twin Oaks Country Inn	(903) 665-3535
Maison Bayou B&B	(903) 665-7600
Mossy Brake Lodge (by Caddo Lake)	(800) 607-6002
Twin Oaks Country Inn	(903) 665-3535
The Black Swan Restaurant	(903) 665-SWAN
Caddo Lake Steamboat Tours	(888) 325-5459

Kerrville, Texas (ERV)/ Fredericksburg, Texas/Gillespie County (T82)

Location: Kerrville sits in the heart of central Texas, the hill country. Fredericksburg is about 25 miles to the northeast of Kerrville.

Airfield: Kerrville Airport, also known as Louis Schreiner Field, is my recommendation for your entry and home base. From here you can enjoy a lovely weekend in the hill country. The longest of two runways, which is 6,000 feet, is wide, smooth, and extremely well maintained. There are no obstacles unmarked or unpredictable. Perhaps the most significant hazard is low-level wind shear created by the undulating hills, which is typical of this region on a warm summer afternoon. The facility's maintenance people do an excellent job of keeping deer from becoming a hazard on the runways. There is no ILS approach, but a variety of nonprecision approaches are available.

If you have an interest in Mooney Aircraft, Schreiner Field is its manufacturing base and headquarters. Tours through the factory are available on request and with prior notification. After hard times and near bankruptcy the company has recently resumed production. Approximately 120 new aircraft are made here each year. I was surprised at the simplicity of operations when I took my tour. It seemed as if each plane was handcrafted, rather than the assembly-line image I had imagined.

Kerrville Aviation is the FBO at the field and it offers excellent service. An Enterprise rental car can be easily arranged for pickup with only short notice. Hangar space is also available.

Schreiner Field is approximately 5 miles from the center of Kerrville, along Route 27.

Fredericksburg is a well-known town, approximately 25 miles from Kerrville, which has maintained a substantial Germanic population and culture since it was founded. The main drawing cards of this small community are quaint shops and antique stores, along with beautifully preserved architecture and municipal buildings. Fredericksburg also has an airfield, although the amenities and services are sparse there in comparison to Kerrville's Schreiner Field. Although the field at Frederickburg (Gillespie County T82) is only 3 miles from town, ground transportation is limited, and taxi service can be unreliable at off-peak

Fredericksburg Airport adjacent to the Pedernales River.

times. The field offers an easy visual approach to the 4,600-foot paved strip with nonprecision approaches available as well.

Attractions:
   State parks, Fredericksburg, bed-and-breakfasts, river activities, ranch activities

Description: Kerrville is perhaps the most well-known and largest small town in the hill country. It is a wonderful place to slow down and pursue those special interests that are so wonderful in this region. There is nothing pretentious about this town and its environs, and the natural beauty is obvious on approach to the airport. As with much of Texas, the summer heat can be stifling, but a nice air-conditioned car to tour the region will provide an adequate haven at this time of year. Several towns are noted for their bed-and-breakfasts, and I would suggest buying a guide if this is a particular interest or focus of yours; otherwise, a few suggestions are provided below.

There is a country elegance about this region and the slow pace is therapeutic, especially if you live in a large city. Kerrville itself has several wonderful places to stay that have reasonable rates. Perhaps the most well-known working ranch is the Y-O Ranch, approximately 20 miles from the center of town. You can be as active a participant in ranch activities as you'd like. Riding, hiking, and even ranch-hand work can be arranged. This is a great getaway and you will shed the hassles of cosmopolitan life on arrival. If you're looking for more action, however, several community festivals occur throughout the year, and these weekends can draw considerable crowds at nearby towns.

When You Go:

Spend a spring or fall weekend around Kerrville. A bit of preparation is well worth your time and will pay dividends in convenience and comfort. For a unique experience, stay at the Y-O Ranch, a genuine working ranch with livestock and virtually all ranch activities. If you would like a home base more akin to a large hotel, easy to get in and out of, then the Y-O Ranch Hotel in the town of Kerrville may be more practical. This place has the nicest restaurant in town as well as a lobby that is comfortable and spacious with stuffed animal heads surrounding you. It is a full-service resort establishment with a pool featuring a swim-up bar. The advantage is convenience, as mentioned, and its attraction is location, not far from major roadways and the center of Kerrville.

Visit the town of Fredericksburg, a 30-minute drive from Kerrville, where you can find a gift or treasure to remind you of your trip in one of the many wonderful shops. Enjoy some strudel and other favorite German delicacies. If you are interested in pursuing the natural splendors of this region, then two suggestions are not far from Fredericksburg. Both of these can be experienced in 2 to 3 hours. The first is Enchanted Rock, some 20 miles north of Fredericksburg. This spectacular piece of granite is within a Texas state park that has been beautifully preserved and is a true natural wonder. It is unspoiled and a terrific place for an afternoon with children or anyone else who would like an invigorating 45-minute hike to the top of the 500-foot peak. The climb is not technically difficult and can be done in tennis shoes. Enchanted Rock is a popular place and in the spring and fall the park will frequently close due to limitations on the number of tourists allowed. Be sure to check prior to making the trek out there. (See contacts.)

Another pleasant spot to pass a few hours of rest and relaxation among the bluebonnets in the spring or the crisp air in the fall is the LBJ Ranch and Nature Preserve. This is east of Fredericksburg on

Route 290, about 10 miles out of town. There are some nature trails surrounding the ranch with wild turkeys, chickens, and other live-stock. This publicly owned reserve is bisected by the Pedernales River and is a wonderful place to picnic as well. There is a visitors center here with facilities and information. Ranch tours are also available.

There are a variety of museums in the area, and these are described in many of the guides to this region.

Contacts:

Kerrville Airport (Louis Schreiner Field)	(830) 257-8000
Fredericksburg Airport	(830) 997-7502
Y-O Ranch	(800) YO-RANCH
Holiday Inn Y-O Ranch Hotel	(830) 257-4440;
	(800) 531-2800
Enchanted Rock State Park	(915) 247-3903
Inn of the Hills River Resort (Kerrville)	(800) 292-5690
Hill Country Museum (in Kerrville)	(830) 896-8633
Taxi Service (Fredericksburg)	(830) 997-6862
Hill Country Lodging and	
Reservation Service	(800) 745-3591
Kerrville Chamber of Commerce	(830) 896-1155
Enterprise Rental Car (Kerrville)	(830) 792-3530
LBJ Ranch and Preserve	(830) 644-2252

Lajitas, Texas (89TE)

Location: Southwest Texas, 50 miles from the Big Bend National Park

Airfield: Lajitas Airport is a privately owned and managed 7,500-foot by 100-foot airstrip 4 miles from the border with Mexico. This strip is now completed and currently in use, but the FBO and facilities were under construction at the time that this entry was written. Although the airport is private, access is granted to virtually all general aviation traffic that requests to use this facility. The field is attended during daylight hours and hangar service is also available. A shuttle service to the resort or center of town at Lajitas is available, efficient and comfortable.

The approach to runway 7 or 25 is strictly VFR, but without major obstacles or hazards. The surrounding area is mountainous, however, with 6,000-foot peaks less than 20 miles away. Please carefully review

The approach to Runway 25 at Lajitas. The backdrop is Mexico.

The author's wife (and model!) perched atop a mesa just outside of the town of Lajitas.

the El Paso sectional chart before arriving. At the time I made my voyage to Lajitas, there was no entry in the Jeppesen database for this airport. The coordinates are longitude north 29°, 16 minutes, and 41 seconds; latitude west 103°, 41 minutes, and 14 seconds. Unicom frequency is 122.9. Perhaps the best way to find Lajitas is by tracking a 225° course from Terlingua Airport, about 14 miles to the northeast. If you cross the Rio Grande, you are in Mexican territory and have gone too far. Another landmark is the Lajitas Resort golf course, 4.2 miles to the southwest of Lajitas Airport. The airport is owned and managed by the resort. If you have an old sectional chart, you will notice that Lajitas Airport was formerly in a different location, designated as a 4,500-foot paved landing surface.

Attractions:

Golf, hiking, mountain-biking, dove hunting, horseback-riding, tennis

Lajitas—an oasis in the heart of Texas' Big Bend area.

Description: Lajitas Resort is a five-star establishment created by the Austin entrepreneur Steve Smith. Smith is still in the process of creating a dream resort, which he calls the "ultimate hideout." After leaving the telecommunications company of Excel, Smith took on Lajitas as a major focus, his project. He actually bought this western town and has transformed it into an oasis for the discriminating sportsman. According to the sales and marketing folks, the goal is to create a community impenetrable to the stresses, hassles, and complications associated with urban and corporate America.

Lajitas Resort features one golf course already. Its rating is 72.9 and the slope is 129, if these numbers mean anything to you. The layout is spectacular: lush green fairways and undulating greens nestled amid the canyons and mesas of this picturesque region. On one hole, you can drive your ball over the border and into Mexico for an attempted hole-in-one. The drawback is that you cannot retrieve your ball, so an alternative hole is reserved for scoring. Greens fees are pricey, as are the majority of services at the resort, approximately $150 per person including cart, weekends and weekdays alike.

Options for dining include an elegant five-star restaurant, which features a variety of exotic game and nouvelle cuisine with a southwestern flair. The ambience is spectacular, and the chef responsible for creating the menu has achieved great fame, winning top awards in Austin over the past two consecutive years. Less formal dining is also available at the resort, and the views and service are equally impressive at this family-style southwestern restaurant overlooking the golf course. A sandwich/ice-cream shop and a cozy bar are located within the main plaza adjacent to the resort.

For the non-golfing sportsman, a dove hunting club, 45 minutes from the resort, complete with comfortable bunk-style accommodations, is planned. Tennis court construction was under way when I visited Lajitas, and a lavish spa is also in the making.

Despite its appeal to upscale clientele, Lajitas maintains its feeling of the Old West. There is a bit of history here, a cavalry post defended by General Pershing in the first part of the last century. The newly erected hotel was built on this site. The rooms are complete with themes that range from Victorian to the Old West and are quite comfortable. The setting is serene and works well with the backdrop of mesas and limestone. The pool and courtyard are tastefully landscaped.

Hiking and horseback riding can be easily arranged any day of the week. The stables are just a few miles from the main resort area.

When You Go:

Take an entourage to Lajitas for a long weekend. Bring your golf clubs and a good pair of walking shoes. The autumn is prime season, as this is desert. Even though the field elevation of Lajitas Airport is 2,600 feet, you are still likely to encounter summer temperatures in the 100s. Bring your camera and a willingness to slow down, unwind, and relax. Very few arrangements are necessary to make before your arrival, as the resort management controls everything in this small town. It is your best resource in planning activities.

Contacts:

Lajitas Resort	(877) LAJITAS;
	(915) 424-5000 (local);
Web site: www.lajitas.com	
For information on	
Big Bend National Park	(915) 477-2291

Lakeway Air Park, Austin, Texas (3R9)

Location: On the southern tip of Lake Travis in the hill country, 18 miles west of Austin

Airfield: This 3,800-foot strip is part of a fly-in community that offers day operations only and follows noise abatement policies. The air park is well maintained, and the runway surface is wide and smooth, but there is a considerable elevation discrepancy between opposite ends of the landing strip in both directions. In other words, the center of the strip is higher than either end, particularly for a landing to runway 16. *Caution:* The air park is a little hard to pick out from a distance, and on the VFR chart its position, with respect to the lake, is your best topographic landmark. A self-serve fuel pump at the tie-down area is easy to use and convenient, but don't count on any airport services other than a phone and a restroom during daylight hours. Touch-and-gos are prohibited, as is night operation.

Attractions:
Golfing, boating, lake side water sports (including sailing school), full marina, tennis, massage/spa/resort setting

Description: Lakeway Air Park is one of the better-known fly-in communities in Texas. This airfield in the hill country offers to the general aviation pilot the opportunity for a wonderful getaway of relaxation and recreation. Clean, prompt, air-conditioned van shuttle service to the Lakeway Resort is available for transport among the resort, airport, and tennis facility regardless of whether you plan to spend a few hours there or the weekend. The resort is situated on the shore of Lake Travis, approximately 2 miles from the landing strip. I have ridden the distance with my foldable bike in about 10 minutes. There are a few hills, but nothing insurmountable, even in the Texas summer heat!

Once you arrive at the resort it's easy to blend in and act like you belong here. I like to sit on the terrace of the lounge overlooking the lake and start the day off with some appetizers or a soft drink. A more formal dining room next to the pub offers a comprehensive brunch, lunch, or dinner if you prefer. You can even sit by the large pool, which is just below the restaurant, and order drinks. Accommodations at the

Lakeway (3R9)

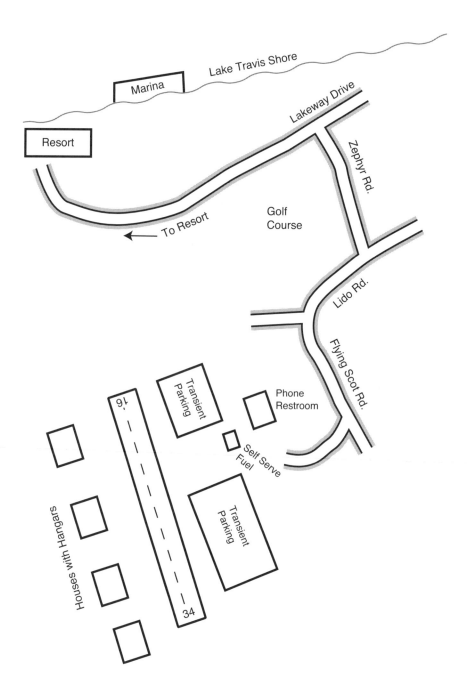

Lakeway resort has a sailing school on site.

resort are quite reasonable—and even a bargain during the off-season. Everything at the resort is right at your fingertips and available for guests. The marina is close to the main building of the resort, below a steep bluff. Although the marina is separately owned, it is affiliated with the resort and offers a wide variety of watercraft rentals to hotel guests and the general public. The rental rate is reduced for guests staying at the hotel.

The tennis facility is closer to the airstrip. This is a large, privately owned club available to guests of the Lakeway resort at a reduced rate. There are indoor and outdoor courts as well a large pool in the shape of a tennis racquet!

Most people know Lakeway for its golf. Two courses are available to guests of the resort, and they are open to the public as well. Greens fees are $50 to $75 per person per round on weekends, including a cart. A third course is a private championship course unavailable even to the guests of the hotel. The two main courses are very nice, not too difficult, and not too crowded.

Lake Travis itself is one of the most popular lakes in Texas. The water is relatively clean and clear, and there are some interesting houses along the shore to marvel at. Some of these mansions are beautifully landscaped and quite impressive in terms of size and architecture. The

Lakeway Resort offers both casual and elegant dining. A view from the pub is shown here.

best way to view the shoreline is by watercraft. Powerboats and wave runners are available from the marina for rent by the hour, half day, or day. On a nice day, in season, reservations are advisable.

Lake Travis is really a portion of the Colorado River that has been dammed up. It leads into the city of Austin but parts are not passable by watercraft secondary to the dams. The portion of Lake Travis at Lakeway is sufficiently wide for sailing. Separate from the Lakeway marina but adjacent to it is a sailing school, where you can charter or rent a sailboat. Sailing lessons are offered as well. On the other side of the marina from the sailing school is a large "riverboat," available most times of the year for dinner or sunset cruises.

When You Go:

Remember to plan your day and to start early if you make a day trip. There are no lights at the airfield and it is restricted to day use

Aerial view of Lakeway Air Park.

only. The shuttle to the resort is reliable; just call the toll-free number from the air park public phone. As you meander through the community to the resort, you will see deer everywhere. Keep this in mind if you are arriving at dusk or dawn as the runway has been known to be a popular loitering location for these creatures.

From the resort, I suggest taking a boat ride or just sitting on the terrace for lunch or brunch on a weekend afternoon. You can really experience the flavor of the lake in a 1- or 2-hour ride and there are several coves to explore not far from the marina for swimming or waterskiing. The golf course is a must for those who want to treat themselves to the management of adversity on grass! Weekend packages are available.

Contacts:

Lakeway Airpark

(512) 261-4385;
(512) 261-6600;

Web site: www.lakewayinn.com

Lakeway Resort	(800) LAKEWAY
Lakeway Marina	(512) 261-7511
Golf Pro Shop	(512) 261-7172
Lakeway Sailing Academy	(512) 261-6193

La Porte, Texas (T41)

Location: La Porte is a "suburb" of Houston just to the southeast of the central city. Kemah is a touristy Gulf-side community, a hot spot for boats and amusement park-style activities, approximately 10 miles from the La Porte airfield on Galveston Bay.

Airfield: La Porte has two intersecting runways, which are wide, smooth, and well maintained. Considering its proximity to Houston, the field has relatively little use and is a great place to practice approaches and landings. Harvey and Rihn Aviation is your best bet for on-site FBO services.

A loaner car is available for short periods, and you can get fuel here as well. Don't expect luxury from the loaner car, but the price is right. I recall borrowing a blue Oldsmobile without air-conditioning in July. Fortunately, my companions were all close friends! Although clearance through Houston's class B airspace can be anxiety-provoking, it is usually not a problem on the weekends and times of light use. VOR and ILS instrument approaches are available.

Attractions:

Gulf-side dining, amusement park style entertainment, shopping

Description: Kemah is a great spot for a day trip of lighthearted fun. This community has been built up over the past 5 to 7 years with dockside restaurants, small shops, and amusement park-type activities. It is a great place to take your children or some friends on a sunny afternoon when the humidity of the Gulf Coast is at its lowest. La Porte Airport is your general aviation gateway to Kemah and easy access to the GA pilot. You only have to flirt with Houston class B airspace and it's possible to skirt underneath to the east to avoid the hassle altogether. As mentioned above, transportation is available and the directions to Kemah from the airport are straightforward.

Although there are places to stay around Kemah and an overnight is possible, you can see most of this small Gulf-side area in an afternoon. This experience is pure entertainment!

When You Go:

Take some friends to Kemah to the dockside restaurant Captain Jack's. Order a whole bunch of appetizers and watch the boats travel back and forth through the channel. This must be the epicenter of flashy cigarette boats, as I have never seen so many fiberglass monsters in my life. They are big and loud and colorful, and the crew are equally flashy—great subjects for people watching. My experiences growing up on Martha's Vineyard in the summer are in complete contradistinction to this scene; nevertheless, I find it wonderfully entertaining. Just walking along the pier is fun and everyone seems to be in a very relaxed mood, friendly, and unrushed. There is a dockside restaurant with an aquarium inside called The Dolphin. It is quite noisy but unique, and a particular attraction to those marine enthusiasts and an eye opener to children.

Contacts:

La Porte Airport	(281) 471-5020
Harvey and Rihn Aviation (FBO)	(281) 471-1675

Laredo, Texas (LRD)

Location: Laredo is a border town, one of the main ports of entry to Mexico

Airfield: Laredo International Airport is a good choice for those general aviation pilots who want to venture into Mexico and enjoy a flavor of that country without taking the possible risk of crossing the border with their aircraft. The field has three large and well-maintained runways to choose from, as well as a variety of precision and nonprecision approaches. The area is wide, flat, and perfect for the student pilot who wants to communicate with the tower yet avoid a high-use and high-stress environment. There are two FBOs at the field, and both provide excellent and courteous service. Labata Aviation usually has plenty of hangar space if you want to pull in your aircraft for the night. The overnight hangar fee is a mere $15. All major rental car agencies are available at the field. The FBO will help facilitate this service as well.

Interestingly, one of the best restaurants in this area is right at the field. It's called Viva Laredo, and the home-cooked meals are outstanding. This place is a must if the timing is right on arrival or departure.

Attractions:
Shopping in Mexico, hunting

Description: Laredo is one of the fastest growing cities in Texas. Undoubtedly, this is secondary to the boost in commerce and trade between the United States and Mexico. Although this destination is not one of the prettier spots on the map or adjacent to one of the more historic or important cities in Mexico, it offers the opportunity to cross the border and enjoy activities and an international atmosphere in a relatively safe and secure environment. Security at the airport is excellent and your aircraft should be well protected without undue or excessive scrutiny from either U.S. or Mexican authorities.

The Mexican town of Nuevo Laredo is a hot spot for many American tourists to enter, score direct retail hits, and enjoy a traditional Mexican meal without an overwhelming fear of gastrointestinal insult! The U.S. town of Laredo, on the other hand, has very little to offer in terms of architecture, natural beauty, amenities, or even historic significance.

There is a traditional central plaza, however, which has been well preserved and is quite charming to walk around. The cathedral at one side of the square is nice.

My recommendations for accommodations include La Posada, a Spanish-style hotel/inn just adjacent to the border and approximately 1-1/2 blocks from the bridge to Mexico. La Posada has two pools with swim-up bars and the ambience and architecture are purely Mexico. Services include a large, air-conditioned shuttle, which will pick you up at the airport at no charge. This obviates the need for a rental car.

Walking into Mexico is a lot easier than driving and less time-consuming as well. As you cross the bridge, approximately 75 yards long, over the Rio Grande and go south of the border, you will see frustrated motorists in line waiting to clear customs. When I went in the summer of 2001, I was not asked to show I.D.; however, a driver's license is reportedly required. The tourist and commercial area in Nuevo Laredo really consists of one main street and a few short side streets. The atmosphere is friendly and relaxed. Street vendors will badger you only to a point and in a very nonthreatening way. There is nothing to fear about visiting this border town if you use some common sense and a bit of courtesy. Bargaining is the rule and be aware that the prices are inflated with the expectation that you will engage in this traditional Mexican commercial activity. Although many of the items are of low quality, you are bound to find some treasures amid the mountains of merchandise. For quality items unique and elegant there are a few shops among the others in the Mercado. Marti's, a specialty store, features fine clothing, jewelry, and collectibles.

Laredo is a southwest Texas haven for hunters during certain seasons. This is a very specialized activity, which I have no experience in, but I know that the area is attractive to those in pursuit of deer and javelina (pronounced ha-vel-*ee*-na). The terrain is dry and the heat can be oppressive, so choose the time of your visit wisely, and consult a local hunting expert if this sport is of interest to you.

When You Go:

Visit Laredo in the fall, winter, or spring and make a reservation at La Posada (ask about reduced off-season rates). Have lunch at the airport shortly after landing and then proceed to the hotel via shuttle van. Venture over the border to Mexico for some retail therapy—be sure to rehearse your bargaining routine beforehand. In Nuevo Laredo, I suggest a festive dinner at Restaurante El Rancho, open daily from noon to midnight. The atmosphere is lively with great tacos, soups, and music.

A visit to the Saint Agustin Church adjacent to the hotel and built in the 1700s is also worthwhile before you leave.

Contacts:

Laredo International Airport	(956) 795-2000
La Posada Inn	(956) 722-1701;
	(800) 444-2099
Viva Laredo	(956) 725-3663
Restaurante El Rancho	011-52-87-14-80-18

Mustang Island—Port Aransas, Texas (2R8)

Location: Gulf Coast on North Padre Island, 20 miles northeast of Corpus Christi

Airfield: Mustang Island is one of the only beachside airports (walkable distance) on the Texas Gulf Coast that I have discovered. Depending on how far from the airport entrance you park or tie down, you may disagree with the term *walkable*. The humidity, temperature, and how much beach paraphernalia you are toting are all factors in this equation. Landing here is easy, however, as the approach is open and the 3,200-foot strip is wide, smooth, and seldom crowded, even on "beach days." Adjacent to the aiport is a marina with restaurant/pub and pool. It's open to the public and offers a variety of refreshments. A shuttle bus leaves from the airport to the town of Port Aransas each hour on the hour for most of the year.

Attractions:
Beach activities, swimming/body surfing, fishing, boating

Description: After exiting the airport drive, the beach is a 10-minute walk along a paved road. The direction is unmistakable and the traffic is usually light. North Padre Island is less well publicized than South Padre, but is comparable in natural splendor. The beachfront abutting the airport is accessible to motor vehicles, and it is possible to drive along the dunes for a short distance. The sand is fine and hard-packed so that four-wheel drive is not necessary, but parking regulations are strictly enforced.

There are few services and amenities available at the beach, so "taking it with you" is advised. There are no waterfront restaurants or hotels, but several are one street back from the water, and various mobile vendors are usually present along the beach frontage. Depending on the time of year, you usually obtain or rent beach chairs, umbrellas, and even surfboards. Food and beverage carts are also seen surfside from time to time throughout the day.

There are a few condominium/rental establishments as you approach the waterfront, just before the beach entrance on the right. One beachside development, named the Island Dunes, has rooms and

Sunscreen is mandatory at Mustang Island!

condominiums for rent at a reasonable rate by the night, weekend, or longer. The town of Port Aransas is about 2 miles from the airstrip. Here you will find numerous options for dining and overnight accommodations. Most of the watersport activities leave from here as well.

The water here is clearer than in Galveston to the north and perhaps not as clear as South Padre to the south; nevertheless, Mustang's beach is clean and a great place to play in the waves with or without your "boogie" board.

When You Go:

A 10- to 15-minute walk to the beach may be just what you need to stretch your legs or it may "break" you if you are laden with picnic supplies in the sweltering August heat. Bring your children and a rig for toting coolers and surfboards. Visit the poolside bar at the marina next to the airport. Enjoy a drink or quick bite here before or after your day at the beach. There is no fuel at Mustang Island, so plan accordingly. Corpus Christi International Airport has reliable services and is

Mustang Island coastline.

easy enough to get in and out of if you need to refuel for the return trip. Mustang Island is your option for a day at the beach without the need for ground transportation.

Contacts:

Mustang Island Airport	(361) 749-4111
Port Aransas Tourist Bureau	(800) 45-COAST
The Island Dunes Condominiums	(361) 749-4923
Woody's Sports Center (boat rides for Port Aransas)	(361) 749-5252
Holiday Inn Gulf Beach Sun Spree Resort	(800) Holiday
Executive Keys Condominiums	(361) 749-6272

New Braunfels, Texas (BAZ)

Location: Approximately 22 miles northeast of San Antonio, in the heart of the hill country

Airfield: New Braunfels Municipal Airport is perhaps the best field in the area for flight training and practice approaches. Three long intersecting runways, combined with ground services but minus commercial activities, make the field ideal for general aviation use, as well as training of pilots. There are rental cars, nearby restaurants, activity around the airport, assistance, and hospitality galore.

Attractions:

Shopping, water sports (river and Schlitterbahn Waterpark), bed-and-breakfast

Description: New Braunfels is a great destination to begin a day trip or weekend in the hill country. New Braunfels is a fairly large town not far from San Antonio. It has some industry, but is surrounded by smaller communities that are more picturesque, quaint, and characteristic of hill-country townships. These destinations are typically Texas and characteristically hill country. New Braunfels Municipal is an excellent airport, but it is by no means your only option. The area is easily accessible from San Antonio International Airport, the closest major commercial field.

One of the challenges in seeking summer activity in Texas is how to stay cool. My quest for adventure, activity, exercise, amusement, and respite from the heat caused me to investigate an activity called tubing. One day, after considerable research, I set out to New Braunfels for an experience that I would like to describe to you. As it was explained to me, I thought tubing was going to be an invigorating and potentially dangerous voyage down stretches of white water and in among sharp rocks and over waterfalls. In one sense, the experience fell short of my expectations, but in another, it was a wonderfully relaxing and refreshing trip that should be experienced on a hot summer day in Texas.

I chose Gruene as a port to begin my tubing expedition. This small town is well known to tourists and offers tremendous hospitality, southern cooking, and wonderful accommodations. Just 200 yards from the main-street intersection in Gruene is the riverside launch of two major tube-rental companies. For those unfamiliar with this activity, tubing

Tubing on the Guadelupe at Gruene, Texas.

is the art of floating down a river on an innertube, or nonmotorized watercraft. You can rent inflatable kayaks or as many innertubes, with or without protective bottoms, that you wish. You can also rent a tube for your cooler or your dog! I recommend the tubes fitted with protective bottoms for those times when the water level is low, that is, mid- to late summer. There are several rivers to choose from in this region. The Guadelupe, which runs through Gruene, is perhaps the most well known. In August, the water temperature is delightful, relaxing yet refreshing. The trip down the short stretch of river takes 2 to 4 hours. You can be as lazy as you want and spend a whole day on the river by rafting up with friends and/or stalling at the slower parts of the river to drink and splash. This activity is great for people of all ages and, as far as I can tell, when the water is relatively low, it offers no considerable major dangers. As always, when alcohol mixes with activity, the potential for poor judgment exists. By and large, everyone was well-behaved when I made my maiden tubing voyage. The majority of folks were college age.

The town of Gruene is a wonderful place to spend a few hours shopping, browsing, or just relaxing. There are numerous antique stores, restaurants, snack bars, and craft shops. Accommodations are mostly bed-and-breakfast-type establishments. The majority are just a walk away from town and, as mentioned, the hospitality was for me and my guests unmatched.

If you are a hardcore shopper, you may be interested in the outlet shops of San Marcos. These are located some 10 miles from New Braunfels, north on Interstate 35. This is a mecca of outlet stores, franchises, and restaurants for the bargain hunter and power shopper.

Not far from New Braunfels airport is the Schlitterbahn. This water park is one of a kind in Texas and a must for those aquaphiles with the longing for an amusement park-type atmosphere. The park is great for fun-loving adults as well as children and worthy of a half-day's commitment at least.

When You Go:

Choose a summer day to travel to New Braunfels. Prearrange a rental car and room (see below). Bring in your four-seater and three friends who characterize themselves as moderately adventurous and water-loving. Take a floatable cooler and proceed to Gruene, following signs to river access points. Use either of the two tubing establishments just on the other side of town. Rental fees, parking, rules of the river, and transportation back to your car are carefully and thoroughly explained upon arrival at Rockin' Rivers Rentals. The people here really have tubing down to a science and nothing is left either to the imagination or to chance. This is a relaxing and safe experience and for me nothing short of baptism into the joys of Texas summer fun!

After tubing, go back to your hotel or bed-and-breakfast, stroll the town of Gruene, and plan to have dinner at the main restaurant in town, called the Grist Mill. On a Friday or Saturday evening, the wait for a table is bound to be lengthy. If you know this is the case, you won't be annoyed but rather entertained by the live music and pleasant riverside surroundings. A tree-filled yard with benches and a full bar made the wait more than tolerable for me and my guests. A band playing folk music and soft rock was the perfect beginning to our evening.

Contacts:

New Braunfels Municipal Airport   (830) 629-1700
Southern Wings Flight Training
    Center (at New Braunfels Airport)   (830) 606-4141

Enterprise Car Rental at the field (830) 629-4522
New Braunfels Chamber of Commerce/
    Visitors Center (800) 572-2626
Schlitterbahn Waterpark (830) 625-2351
Rockin' Rivers Adventure Tube Rental (888) 88-FLOAT
Grist Mill Restaurant (in Gruene) (830) 625-0684
Gruene Apple Inn (830) 643-1234

Useful Web site: www.nbjumpin.com

Possum Kingdom/Graford, Texas (F35)

Location: Possum Kingdom Airfield is in the community of Graford, 60 miles to the west of Fort Worth just into the hill country

Airfield: The airstrip at Possum Kingdom is wide, smooth, and an excellent area to practice approaches, touch-and-gos, and safety maneuvers. Most of the time it's very quiet here, but on weekends you'll find some people at the airfield, particularly during the summer. The visual approach is straightforward and good landmarks include the lake to the west and a nearby hill to the southeast. After you land, recognize that ground transportation is quite limited here and self-sufficiency is advised. The municipal airport terminal building has little more than a restroom and a telephone. No fuel is available.

Attractions:
   Fishing, camping, biking, wildflowers, water sports

Description: Possum Kingdom is a recreational area, a community built largely around the lake, which resulted from damming up the Brazos River. This is a favorite fishing lake and many folks choose to camp here for a weekend or a few days. The many fingerlike projections of the lake make its lengthy coastline interesting and uniquely private. Commercial activities in Possum Kingdom are scarce, as is ground transportation around the airport. This is one of the problems when you fly in here, as there is no taxi service. Foldable bicycles in your plane can solve this problem. However, in the springtime, the wildflowers around the airport are quite beautiful and a Sunday-afternoon walk will make you feel miles away from any big city. People in the airport community are out working in their yards and the local hospitality is typically southern, something I have grown to appreciate, coming from New England. The surrounding area is quiet with rolling hills and beautiful pastures.

   There is a hilltop to the southeast, which I discovered one afternoon while riding my bicycle. An organization had erected a cross on top of a huge platform overlooking Possum Kingdom Lake. I can't think of a more beautiful place for a picnic and I've returned to it more than once. I'm not sure whether this is private land, but no one has ever bothered

Possum Kingdom (F35)

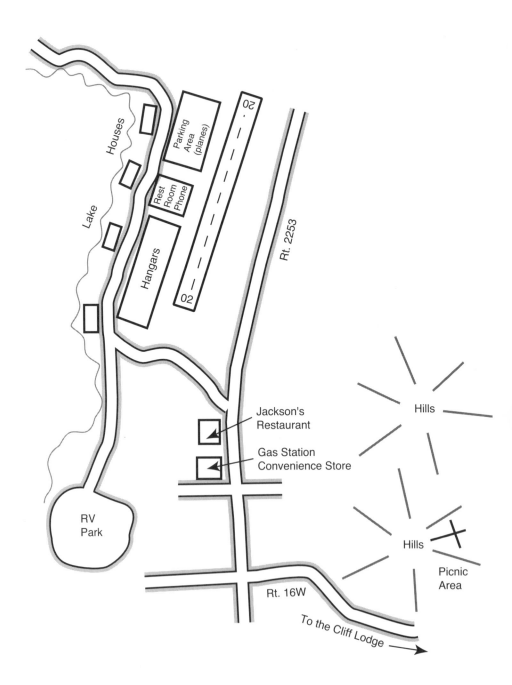

A view from the grounds of the Cliff Lodge, Possum Kingdom.

me or suggested I was trespassing. *Caution:* The climb to this lookout can be a vigorous journey in the Texas summer heat.

Approximately 3 miles from the airstrip is a public boat ramp and marina at Possum Kingdom. This is an area for swimming, fueling watercraft, and wave-runner rentals called Fundock (see contacts). About 8 miles from the airfield is a wonderful resort called The Cliff. This establishment is a lakeside resort with all the amenities including an eighteen- hole golf course, tennis courts, and water-sport rentals, boats, and wave-runners. A courtesy van will provide shuttle service to and from the airport.

Even if you're not looking for a simple day or afternoon trip, Possum Kingdom is perfect. Approximately 1 mile from the runway is a great spot for brunch, lunch, or a family-style dinner. Jackson's offers traditional homestyle Texas cooking. Most of the clientele are families and bass fishermen. The walls are decorated with trophy fish, including a 300-pound sailfish. I'm sure this critter is a transplant, just like me, and not a native of the lake! Jackson's is a leisurely walk from the airport along a relatively quiet road.

A view from the author's favorite picnic spot, Possum Kingdom.

When You Go:

Choose a spring morning to fly to Possum Kingdom, pack a picnic lunch, and if possible take your bicycles. Visit my favorite picnic spot up on the hill overlooking the lake (see map). Enjoy the wildflowers and think about world peace or, better yet, nothing at all. On your way back to the airport, stop at Jackson's and have an iced tea and a burger. Wear your baseball hat and your bass fishing T-shirt and blend in with the crowd.

Contacts:

Possom Kingdom Airport	(940) 779-2321
Jackson's Restaurant	(940) 779-4131
Fundock (wave-runner rental)	(940) 779-3737
The Cliff Resort and Condominiums	(940) 779-3625

Smithville, Texas (84R)

Location: A small town in central Texas, 40 miles east of Austin

Airfield: Smithville Municipal Airport consists of a 3,200-foot paved strip with a small, newly erected and well-air-conditioned lounge/office. A few hangars surround the field and there is some ultra-light activity as well. Make no mistake, it's very quiet here and a great place to practice approaches and touch-and-gos. The airport area is quite open and should not pose any significant or unexpected difficulties in the way of hazards to a visual approach.

Attractions:
　　Mountain biking at Rocky Hill Ranch, camping at the state recreational facility

Description: I've included Smithville especially for a stay at the Rocky Hill Ranch and for the off-road cycling fanatic. This is really a neat place to visit, however, even if you don't want to beat yourself up on this course, which draws mountain bikers from all over the state, particularly those serious racing types from Austin.

　　Rocky Hill Ranch is approximately 2-1/2 miles from the Smithville airfield. This is a privately owned spread of land primarily used for camping and off-road cycling. Periodically, races are held that gain state, if not national, acclaim. Just inside the entrance to the ranch is the Rocky Hill Saloon. This is an establishment well worth a look. It has great veggie burgers and hamburgers, not to mention a full complement of beverages. Many local folks like to hang out here who have no interest in cycling. In fact, I distinctly remember that half of the clientele were smoking unfiltered Camel cigarettes and the other half were slurping on protein shakes while comparing their latest experiences in body piercing. What was more amazing was how well these two groups melded together beneath the eclectic decor of the saloon. This place is a must!

　　For the serious off-road cyclist, there is an extensive network of off-road trails that wind through the ranch. Some of the trails are technical, but high-speed cruising is possible through much of the other terrain. The trails are well marked and water is provided strategically around the course. The price for using the trails is $8 per person. Helmets are mandatory and maps are provided. The folks who run and

Smithville (84R)

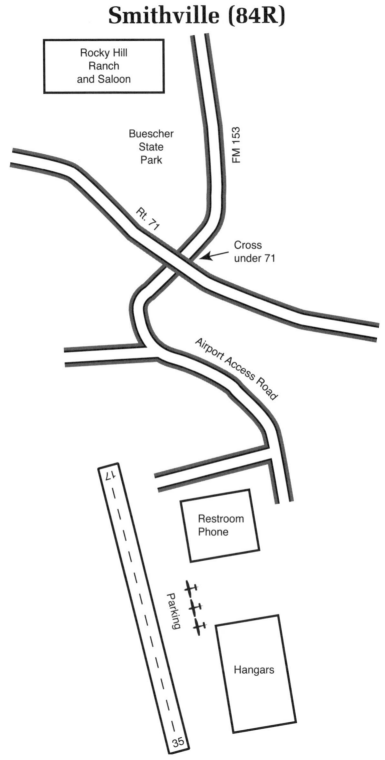

Ultralight at Smithville Airport.

maintain the trails staff the saloon as well, and they are extremely courteous and helpful. You can have a shower at the saloon after your ride, but don't expect luxury, only the basics. Bring your own towels.

Alternatively, there is a state park for noncyclist campers about 1 mile on the left before the ranch. Overnight camping is permitted.

When You Go:

Pack your mountain bikes and head to Rocky Hill Ranch (see map). Plan on lunch at the Rocky Hill Saloon and bring a change of clothes. Don't forget your helmet and towel. The saloon keepers will guard your belongings while you bike. Call about trail conditions before you make the trip.

Contacts:

Smithville Municipal Airport	(512) 237-2582
Rocky Hill Ranch and Saloon	(512) 237-3112

South Padre Island

Texas/Brownsville International (BRO)
Port Isabel, Texas/Cameron County (T31)
Harlingen, Texas (HRL)

Location: South Padre Island is in the southernmost portion of Texas on the Gulf Coast. It is a long peninsula that divides the intercoastal waterway from the Gulf.

Airfield: The island is accessible from at least three airfields. The small municipal field, Port Isabel, is closest to the island but offers the fewest amenities and facilities. Port Isabel is wide open and instrument approaches are available, both GPS and ILS. The three intersecting runways are well maintained, wide, and smooth. The FBO at the field is Southwind Aviation and these folks are very helpful. Hangar space is available. Security is excellent for a small airport because of a nearby correctional facility. A rental car must be arranged in advance (see below).

Harlingen is perhaps the most popular general aviation field, some 25 miles to the west. Southwest Airlines uses this facility as well. The GA area is separate from the main terminal. Rental cars can be picked up here seven days a week.

Brownsville International Airport services several commercial airlines and is approximately 20 miles to the south. The two FBOs here are within walking distance of the main terminal. Both offer friendly line service with conveniences, in addition to reliable security. Brownsville International Airport is a wonderful place to mix it up with the "big guys." This is a typical "international airport" that is quite sleepy and gets very little international traffic. The controllers are relaxed and helpful. There is nothing to fear about landing here if you are an inexperienced pilot. BAC, or Brownsville Air Center, is the first FBO you'll see as you turn off runway 17-35 toward the north end of the ramp. This establishment offers kind and courteous service, but is farther away from your rental car than Hunt Aviation, which is adjacent to the main terminal. As one would expect with any major airport, Brownsville offers every kind of approach as well as small restaurants and all of the big rental car companies. The runways are long and wide and the taxiway system is straightforward.

Sandcastles at South Padre Island.

Attractions:

Fishing (charter, pier), boating, sailing, wind surfing, beach activities, birding

Description: South Padre Island is notorious during college spring break; best to enjoy the island's serenity and natural beauty the rest of the year. It is not difficult to avoid the crowds, given the length of available beach, with just a little initiative. The most accessible waterfront is lined by large hotels and condominiums, but the beach is remarkably clean and well maintained during most of the year.

There are a wide variety of restaurants in South Padre and accommodations can be found for any length of stay. As suggested above, this place takes on an entirely different flavor when you are not there during peak season. Choose your visit to suit your needs and you won't be disappointed. If peace and quiet and long walks on the beach are what you desire, I would go anytime from October to March. If you are looking for a more vibrant experience with night life and beach parties, April, May, and June are the best months to make the scene.

When You Go:

Affordable accommodations are usually available year round, but during the busy spring and summer months reservations are strongly advised. In the off-season, you can be more casual about planning ahead and even chance just looking around without reservations. Accommodations will range in price depending how close you want to be to the beach and whether you want a condominium or a standard hotel. Some recommendations are listed below. In the off season, it should be noted that discounts are the rule. If there is no mention of this, inquire of the management.

Amberjacks is a nice luncheon spot when you first arrive on the island. It's on the intercoastal waterway side, your left side, as you drive onto the island and turn toward the south. The fish specials are mouthwatering and the backyard terrace offers a great view. You can sit outside and watch the fishing boats, windsurfers, and wave runners as they share the bay in front of you. The atmosphere is relaxed and even a bit tropical.

If you have ever wanted to take a bicycle ride on the beach, this is your best bet for a long and relatively easy ride. The sand is hard-packed and the beach is wide with plenty of room to avoid the bathers and children. This beach is also great for flying kites or making sand castles; it's a real family place. I rode my Dahon foldable bike on the sand several miles without much effort.

At the end of the beach, to the north, you will find a long jetty lined with fishermen. Even if you are not a fisherman, it is fun to watch those who are reeling in their catch. All along the beach you can rent rafts, bicycles, body surfing boards, beach chairs and so on.

South Padre Drive is the main street. It's set back from the beach and runs parallel to it. This road is lined with surf shops, and cycle and dune-buggy rentals, as well as restaurants and convenience stores. For breakfast, try Rovan's on the Gulf side of the main strip about 2 miles from the bridge. This is an institution with more choices for breakfast than you could imagine; I loved the pecan waffles with a healthy dollop of whipped cream. Several fun and casual seafood spots are listed below. Joseph's is one of the nicer, more romantic places for a candlelight dinner, close to the water.

Contacts:

Brownsville Air Center	(956) 542-5572
FBO at Brownsville International Airport	(956) 542-5572
Harlingen Airport	(956) 430-8600

FBO at Port Isabel   (956) 233-4424

Accommodations on South Padre Island—Central Agencies:
Island Services   (800) 426-6530;
                                         (956) 761-2649
Padre Island Rentals/Island
   Reservation Services   (800) 926-6926;
                                         (956) 761-5653
Condos:
   Padre Island Rentals   (800) 926-6926
   Padre Island Reservation Service   (800) 943-5424
Restaurants:
   Rovan's Restaurant and Bakery   (956) 761-3930
   Joseph's Restaurant and Bar   (956) 761-4540
Fishing (charter)
   Jim's Pier   (956) 761-2865
   Fisherman's Wharf   (956) 761-7818
   Sea Ranch Marina   (956) 761-5493
   Captain Murphy   956-761-2764
Recreational water sports
   (sailing, kayaks, wind surfing)   (956) 761-5061
   The Boatyard on Dolphin Street   956-761-5061;
                                         800-408-8396
Over sand vehicle rental   956-761-9273
For sailboats, kayak, windsurfing—
   The Boatyard   (956) 761-5061;
   (800) 408-8396
For over sand vehicle rentals—
   Island Fun Rentals   (956) 761-9273

Appendix 1

Geographical List

Appendix 2

Attractions List

Lakeside

Seaside/Beach

Mountains

Museums/Historic

Amusement/Shopping

Fishing/Hunting/Camping

Sports (golf, tennis, and biking)